The Politically Correct Christian

Trading Christ Centeredness for Political Correctness

Mark Taylor

Copyright © 2014 Mark Taylor

All rights reserved.

ISBN-10: 1532781237
ISBN-13: 978-1532781230

DEDICATION

I would like to dedicate this book to my wife who has helped make this book a reality.

CONTENTS

Acknowledgments   i

Introduction

1 The PCC in the Home   21

2 The PCC and the Government   47

3 The PCC in the School System   69

4 The PCC in the Church   87

5 The PCC in the Community   115

6 The PCC in the Work Place   135

7 The PCC and Money   159

8 The PCC in Relationships   181

Conclusion   213

ACKNOWLEDGMENTS

I would like to acknowledge Jenna Vreugdenhil in helping with the book cover graphics, Lauren Batchelor and to Rachel Boice for their help in the editing process. I would also like to thank all my friends, family and churches for the help and input throughout this writing process.

INTRODUCTION

The media in today's society preaches about acceptance, tolerance and "political correctness." This philosophy has become a hot topic for many. It can be easy for us as Christians and citizens of the United States of America to start believing and even allowing such unbiblical types of behavior and thought to creep into our lives. Not that we are to reject all of what society says, but we must filter everything through God's Word and view this world through God's eyes.

My desire is that this book be a help in our Christian walk through life. I pray this book is encouraging, challenging, funny and helpful. Romans 3:23 says, For all have sinned and fall short of the glory of God. We have all, in our daily walks through life, fallen short and missed the mark of living the Christian life; some struggle in certain areas and others do not. This book is meant to help, guide, encourage, and challenge us in specific areas of our lives that we all experience at one point or another.

Please keep Romans 3:23 in the back of your mind as you read through the book. We are all sinners and we all mess up in our lives, myself included. However, as children of

God, we are to continue serving God and following after Him. I pray that this book be a help and platform of discussion and base for spiritual growth, realizing that as you read this, I am taking what God's Word says and helping to apply it to our lives.

It is my desire and prayer that we open our eyes and recognize when we are following the social norms rather than following what God has commanded. I am burdened for Christians in America, as we are bombarded with so much information, true and false, that we lose sight of what we are to do and who we are to follow.

Well meaning, educated, and authoritative people use words like weapons in order to push their ideas, personal opinions, and even their own agenda of ethics and morals. They often use limited human understanding as building blocks for society's laws, rules, and lifestyle. Anyone who would challenge these thoughts and ideas of the "well meaning, educated, and authoritative people" would be cut down by the onslaught of verbal labels such as bigot, extremist, radical, rebel, and so on.

In truth, who would want to challenge such pillars of society? Would any of us want to be considered intolerant and non-accepting? If we are politically incorrect, will it affect our jobs, our friends, family, or life? Why risk it? Just go with the flow, right? After all, these people are paid six-figure salaries or more to know what's best for us. Their weapons of words and cheap philosophy can soon control our lives, society, economy, religious, and global perspective.

I would like to define and establish some of these terms that are used so that we may all be on the same page, so to speak.

> **Acceptance**: Merriam-Webster's Dictionary defines this as, "*Agreeing either expressly or by conduct to the act or offer of another.*"[1]

If we were all Bible-believing Christians, this would not be a problem. Unfortunately, this is not the case. America, dubbed the great melting pot of culture, has taken it upon itself to lower the standards.[2] Along with the lowering of our standards as a society, we have also forgotten the most fundamental things that our Founding Fathers built this great country on, religious freedom.

Although they do not teach it in history books or in public schools, our Founding Fathers knew and feared God, and that is why this country is, or was, so great.

---

[1] *Merriam-Webster's Collegiate Dictionary,* s.v. "Acceptance."
[2] Basic math illustrates that in order to get everything equal, you must lower everything to the lowest common denominator. That is fine in math, not in life. Instead of lowering everything, why not elevate? Does God lower His standards? No!

We have gone from standing for what we know is right, to cowering and essentially bowing to the wishes of a few that complain in the name of acceptance.

This kind of "preaching" that the media instills upon us is wrong. Under this doctrine of acceptance, and by this definition, we are to be in agreement with them. When you agree with someone, does it not mean that you condone or approve and make it acceptable? Then it would stand to reason that, just on this term alone, we could or would be going against what the Bible says and what the Christian faith holds to. Let's see what the next term has in store for us.

> **Tolerance:** Merriam-Webster defines this as *sympathy or indulgence for beliefs or practices differing from or conflicting with one's own; the act of allowing something.*[3]

Let's look at an example of what Jesus thought related to the topic of tolerance.

> In Matthew 21:12-16 it says, "And Jesus entered the temple and drove out all who sold and bought in the temple, and He overturned the tables of the money-changers and the seats of those who sold pigeons. He said to them, "It is written, 'My house shall be called a house of prayer,' but you make it a den of robbers. And

---

[3] *Merriam-Webster's Collegiate Dictionary,* s.v. "Tolerance."

the blind and the lame came to Him in the temple, and He healed them. But when the chief priests and the scribes saw the wonderful things that He did, and the children crying out in the temple, 'Hosanna to the Son of David!' they were indignant, and they said to Him, 'Do you hear what these are saying?' And Jesus said to them, "Yes; have you never read, 'Out of the mouth of infants and nursing babies you have prepared praise?'"

Focus your attention on verses 12 and 13 where Jesus overturns tables. That doesn't sound like a very tolerant person to me. I am not saying we should be outraged over everything, but it does show that there can be righteous anger, especially when it involves our beliefs.[4] Stop for a moment and ask yourself, how lazy is your faith?

How lackadaisical is the Christian Church across America? Are we as believers taking the easy road by being tolerant and ignoring issues in our community, churches, and lives? Are we willing to step up and do what is needed, what is commanded? Can you get righteously angry as the sin that surrounds us? Or is your goal to just get by in life and be "politically correct" to survive and thrive?

---

[4] To be clear, this is not giving you permission to whip people in your church because they do not believe the same as you. Just because you believe that there should be coffee and doughnuts and another believes there should be water and fat free organic rice cakes is not a reason to begin whipping and tossing stuff around.

Being politically correct can go against what the Bible teaches. We are to stand firm in what we believe, in love with all kindness and gentleness.[5] There are numerous verses about how a believer should stand firm in what the scripture teaches. We cannot look at them all right now, but I will strive to hit on them throughout this book.

If we were to allow something that we knew was wrong, wouldn't that be the same as condoning it or even being a part of it? Imagine if a person were to start juggling loaded hand guns with the safety off in a very crowded room, and they had never had a juggling lesson in their life. Imagine you were the only person in the room to have this information, yet you did nothing about it. Wouldn't that be the same as condoning their actions?

By doing nothing, you are, in essence, accepting and allowing that kind of behavior to happen, by being tolerant of that person's stupidity and disregard for others' safety. In legal terms, you could be an accessory to this tragedy. You could/would be responsible for their deaths and injuries.[6]

In this line of thinking, I am reminded of a quote that is often attributed to Sir Edmund Burke but has also been used by many other people. That is: "The only thing necessary for the triumph of evil is that good men do nothing."

---

[5] Ephesians 6:10-18
[6] James 4:17

The question then begs to be asked, are you a good person? Are you willing to stand by and do nothing?

Scary thought, right? When we begin to see how our actions can impact not just ourselves but those around us whom we love and care about, we must take caution. Like the person trying to juggle loaded handguns in a crowded room, how much more dangerous is it when we allow people to try and juggle with their eternal souls? Will we be complacent? Accessories to their spiritual tragedy? All for what? Tolerance?

Moving on from acceptance and tolerance, there is another word that I think would be beneficial for us to understand: propaganda. This word is often not used anymore, but in reality, is being implemented around us 24/7.

> **Propaganda**: Merriam-Webster says that Propaganda is *the spreading of ideas, information, or rumor for the purpose of helping or injuring an institution, a cause, or a person.*[7]

Now, when you think about this definition logically, you cannot just help one institution without hurting another institution. For example, the government gives over 500 million taxpayer dollars a year to Planned Parenthood.[8] This

---

[7] *Merriam-Webster's Collegiate Dictionary*, s.v. "Propoganda."
[8] *Planned Parenthood Annual Report 2012-2013*. Report. New

can and does hurt the little, church-funded, right-to-life organizations.

How can a small, right-to-life organization try to compete against such a giant organization with funding and recognition like Planned Parenthood? How can these right-to-life clinics offer free classes and have the resources to offer? How can they go into schools to pass out material showing all the alternatives? Can they even afford campaigns and national advertisements illustrating the importance and sanctity of life?

We hear how "good" Planned Parenthood is for our country, but they neglect to inform us about how many abortions are performed and little precious lives are snuffed out every year. How many pregnancy prevention items are handed out so that our children can engage in debauchery?

Some believe that propaganda started in the early years of World War I, but they are strongly misled. The battle for the people's minds started as far back as time. Remember Adam and Eve? Satan tried to convince Eve that the fruit would be okay to eat and that God wouldn't punish her?[9] Skip ahead to the Roman Empire. Although they didn't have newspapers, radio, or TV, they did have such things as plays,

---

York: Planned Parenthood, 2013.
http://www.plannedparenthood.org, 18.

[9] Genesis chapter 3

dramas, games, laws, and religious festivals. Through public events such as these, the Roman Empire could sway popular thought from one side to the other.

In today's society, it is far easier to run the propaganda machine than ever before, yet we, as Christians and as a society, let them with little or no resistance. With so many media outlets attacking us at any given time, we sit back and allow them to fill our hearts, minds, and homes with their information.

The secular world view is anything but Christian, and your mind can't help but be bombarded by the secular and unbiblical viewpoints. Pause for a second and take a long hard look at how this worldview influences you as a person, an adult, a parent, a Christian. Is this the plan that God has for us? The answer is No.

An example of secular propaganda is what has been done to women between the ages of 14 and 24[10]. Think with me for a second. Instead of pushing purity, reserve, knowledge, and wisdom on these women, they push romance, sex, and sex appeal with a whole host of other damaging, demoralizing, unfulfilling and frankly, unobtainable false goals. It is no wonder that there is such promiscuity among our young women today. I have seen the statistics;

---

[10] I have a friend who teaches fifth grade, and it is already being presented to them at that age.

while teenage pregnancy is down,[11] birth control is also more readily available.[12] [13]

What are we allowing in our homes, beliefs, thoughts, and lives? How could this happen? What have we done or not done to get to this point? There is still one more definition that I would like to look at before we move on.

> **Political Correctness**: Merriam-Webster defines political correctness as *conforming to a belief that language and practices which could offend political sensibilities (as in matters of sex or race) should be eliminated*[14]

I know you are sitting there reading and thinking, "Yeah, so what? It's not that bad." But let's think about this for a second. The last part of that definition states that any belief or language that could offend someone should be eliminated. Elimination does not sound good to me, and as a Christian, we are to not conform to the world.

---

[11] U.S. Census Bureau (2010) Retrieved from http://www.census.gov/2010census/.
[12] *Planned Parenthood Annual Report 2012-2013*. Report. New York: Planned Parenthood, 2013. http://www.plannedparenthood.org, 10.
[13] It should be noted as well that anal and oral sex are more prominent among the youth today, thus allowing them to have sex but not get pregnant. However, many youth believe and consider those two ways as not even having sex, thus they can participate in such acts and still be a "virgin."
[14] *Merriam-Webster's Collegiate Dictionary*, s.v. "Political Correctness."

Romans 12:2 says, "Do not be conformed to this world, but be transformed by the renewal of your mind, that by testing you may discern what is the will of God, what is good and acceptable and perfect."

If we are not conforming to the world and we are standing out as followers of Christ, then logically speaking, we will be offending someone. If we are offending someone or a group of people, then by the definition of political correctness, we should be eliminated.

What happened to freedom of speech and right to religious practice? Did our country trade in our freedom of speech for political correctness?

Please do not misunderstand me. I am not trying to start a fight or incite people to be rude and consciously offensive.[15] However, I am trying to bring home this thought, as believers and followers of Christ, our very actions, behavior, and speech would/should/could be offensive as we try to obey the commands of God's Word.

When and where did all of this start? According to "The Origins of Political Correctness," An Accuracy in Academia address by Bill Lind. Bill starts out by saying,

> *Where does all this stuff that you've heard about this morning – the victim feminism, the gay rights movement, the invented statistics,*

---

[15] Colossians 3:8, 4:6

the rewritten history, the lies, the demands, all the rest of it – where does it come from? For the first time in our history, Americans have to be fearful of what they say, of what they write, and of what they think. They have to be afraid of using the wrong word, a word denounced as offensive or insensitive, or racist, sexist, or homophobic.

We have seen other countries, particularly in this century, where this has been the case. And we have always regarded them with a mixture of pity, and to be truthful, some amusement, because it has struck us as so strange that people would allow a situation to develop where they would be afraid of what words they used. But we now have this situation in this country. We have it primarily on college campuses, but it is spreading throughout the whole society. If we look at it analytically, if we look at it historically, we quickly find out exactly what it is. Political Correctness is cultural Marxism. It is Marxism translated from economic into cultural terms. It is an effort that goes back not to the 1960's and the hippies and the peace movement, but back to World War I.[16]

The term "political correctness" started out as a joke -- literally, it was found in a comic strip.[17] Even today, people still take it very lightheartedly, but it is not funny. While we laugh, the political correctness machine is running and infiltrating our country, colleges, work place, homes, and lives.

---

[16] Bill Lind, "The Origins of Political Correctness," *Accuracy in Academia* (2000), http://www.academia.org/the-origins-of-political-correctness/.
[17] Ibid.

For far too long we have sat in our comfy chairs and been pushed around, fearing that we might offend someone with our beliefs. We have been fed this line that, as Christians, we need to just be quiet and take what the world throws at us. Be tolerant, be silent, be understanding, be permissible, be what the world wants us to be.

I can say, without a doubt in my mind, that God would not condone this kind of action or behavior. How many Christians do you know that are sideline Christians not wanting to get into the game? Perhaps you know Christians who are so afraid of offending someone that they don't say or act the way they should.

If we were to look at a group of people, how would you be able to tell who was and who wasn't a Christian? Would you be one counted for Christ? Or would you be the one that blended in with the rest of the worldly population?

I am not saying that all Christians should wear WWJD T-shirts and sing Kumbaya all the live long day. However, we should be able to stand out and people should see Christ through our lives and by our actions.

As stated earlier in Romans 12:2, Paul talks about how we shouldn't be conformed to this world but be transformed. We are to impact the world in which we live, not be impacted. We are to set the standard, not just follow it. We are to transform, not conform to this world.

Before moving on, let's address the issue of transformation. Who are we to transform into? What are we to become if we are not to conform? The answer is simple yet very difficult. We are to become more like Christ every single day. We will never be perfect this side of heaven, but we are to strive our hardest to transform into the children of God that He has called us to be.

Conformed means to be identical or similar to, even become obedient to. How can a person conform to Jesus yet try and fit in with the world? Imagine trying to get a large SUV to conform to a little sports car, you chop and swap and try your hardest to get it to look like a sports car. But at the end of the day, it is still an SUV that is trying to conform to that image.[18]

When you think of being conformed as being obedient, it brings a whole new meaning to the verse found in Luke 16:13 that says,

> No servant can serve two masters, for either he will hate the one and love the other, or he will be devoted to the one and despise the other. You cannot serve God and money.

---

[18] How many times do you or I try and change our image to become something or someone we are not? We try and change how and who God made us to be.

We cannot conform to one without hating the other. It is an all or nothing reality that we as believers need to understand and own.

On the positive side, you do not really need to worry too much about being politically incorrect. Take a look at the life of Jesus; He was not concerned about being politically correct. For example, when the Pharisees came to Jesus, they were upset because He was allowing His disciples to work on the Sabbath, which wasn't allowed in the Jewish law.

Talk about being politically incorrect. In Matthew 12:8, Jesus responds to the accusation that the Son of Man is Lord of the Sabbath.

I must warn you that there could be some heat, some backlash, some suffering, and some tough decisions from following Jesus' example. Jesus even warns us in Matthew 10:16-26,

> Behold, I am sending you out as sheep in the midst of wolves, so be wise as serpents and innocent as doves. Beware of men, for they will deliver you over to courts and flog you in their synagogues, and you will be dragged before governors and kings for my sake, to bear witness before them and the Gentiles. When they deliver you over, do not be anxious how you are to speak or what you are to say, for what you are to say will be given to you in that hour. For it is not you who speak, but the Spirit of your Father speaking through you.
> Brother will deliver brother over to death, and the father

his child, and children will rise against parents and have them put to death, and you will be hated by all for my name's sake. But the one who endures to the end will be saved. When they persecute you in one town, flee to the next, for truly, I say to you, you will not have gone through all the towns of Israel before the Son of Man comes. A disciple is not above his teacher, nor a servant above his master. It is enough for the disciple to be like his teacher, and the servant like his master. If they have called the master of the house Beelzebub, how much more will they malign those of his household.

Although we may experience some negative repercussions as we strive to follow after Jesus and not this world, I can assure you that it will be worth it. Not only will it be worth it, but we are commanded to in the Great Commission and it is in our very DNA as believers.

We are to strive and seek after the heart of God as we obey and love Him with our hearts, souls, bodies, and minds.[19]

In this book we are going to look at some very important areas in our lives where we are pushed into being politically correct and how we should act, live, and respond as Christians. Remember, we are all sinners and imperfect, we all mess up, and we are all trying to follow God and His Word.

---

[19] Matthew 22:37

Please be honest with yourself as you read. You do not have to air out your dirty laundry to everyone, but be honest with yourself. Allow this book to be a guide, a help, an easy read to remind us of how we are to follow after God. I pray that you will get as much out of reading as I have gotten out of writing *The Politically Correct Christian*.

Mark Taylor

1
THE POLITICALLY CORRECT CHRISTIAN IN THE HOME

Oh, for the days of yesteryear, the white picket fence, the perfectly manicured yard, the smell of freshly made bread and cookies. Let's not forget the two or three perfect, obedient little children. You walk into the house with the dog greeting you with a wagging tail and your children greet you with a hug and kiss announcing that they have already finished their homework.

Dinner is almost on the table, but you have a few extra minutes to love your spouse and relax. After dinner you have family time, play a board game and then the children go right upstairs to prepare for bed, quickly drifting off to sleep.

Be honest, we all long for this kind of life. And why wouldn't we? It happens in Hollywood. Haven't you seen *Leave it to Beaver* or *The Andy Griffith Show*? If it can happen there, then why can't it happen in our house as well, right? Wrong!

Obviously those shows have writers, and our lives are just not scripted like that. In all seriousness though, a prevailing theme that gets brought up in homes today is that of discipline.

One of the problems in today's society and in our homes is the lack of discipline. But why should there be any discipline? After all, I never saw them spank a kid on TV. The Hollywood parents would have a nice talk to their children explaining how not to do it. Or the child would do something wrong, the child would apologize, everyone gets a good laugh and life was great. Well, that is television, not real life.

Sadly though, more and more people watch TV expecting that their home life should mimic the well-written scripts and shows we spend hours watching. When this "TV expectation" is not met, often the temptation is to leave and find a new home in hopes of finding and meeting this false expectation.

Discipline is a main, if not *the* key function to having a great home life. However, with the trends of society moving towards being accepting of any and all kinds of behavior, the act of discipline is being looked down upon and quickly becoming a thing of the past. When discipline is lost, there is a break down in the home. If a parent does not discipline their children, then it can do more harm than good.

Proverbs 13:24 says, "Whoever spares the rod hates his son, but he who loves him is diligent to discipline him."

Hebrews 12:11 says, "For the moment all discipline seems painful rather than pleasant, but later it yields the peaceful fruit of righteousness to those who have been trained by it."

Proverbs 23:13-14 says, "Do not withhold discipline from a child;   if you strike him with a rod, he will not die. If you strike him with the rod, you will save his soul from Sheol (death)."

We will look at a few of these in more depth later in the chapter.

Discipline is a great way of instructing and training. Think with me for a moment, how good would our military be if they decided to stop disciplining their soldiers? What if they wanted to be more sensitive to the soldiers' needs and make sure they were comfortable, rather than train and discipline them to competence? What would happen when a war broke out? What would happen when things got tough or hard times came?

Like a soldier, Christians are in a spiritual war. We all need discipline so that when the time comes, we will be prepared. This truth is even more important within the home. We must discipline and prepare our children so that when life gets hard and/or when the time comes, they can stand up for what is right and be able to withstand the onslaught of life's trials and win the spiritual war.

There have been many incidents in recent history of parents trying to discipline their children. The end result was their children being taken away from their home, parents and family.[20] Before getting too carried away, I recognize and understand that there are situations that require such measures, but I also believe that it can happen too often and not when it is needed.

Society, in an attempt to "protect," has designed organizations to come down on parents to a point that parents are afraid to discipline their own kids. The result of this is that there is no respect for parents or authority figures in general. Combine this type of mentality with well-meaning people who can overreact, pull out of context, misunderstand, or attempt to enforce their individual viewpoints by simply making an anonymous phone call to the organization, and parents have legitimate reasons to fear.

We would be foolish to think that children do not understand how this system works. Public schools, child

---

[20] I have seen this first hand in several accounts and know of other such incidents across the country. There is a fine line between discipline and abuse, those lines should never cross. However society has taken the liberty of trying to merge these two terms into synonyms.

specialists, and numerous books avidly preach about spanking and other forms of discipline as wrong. This, consequently, allows and gives the children authority over the parents.

One wrong disciplinary action and the parents could find themselves in jail and without their children. How can a parent be a parent when they are scared to death of what could happen to them if they needed to discipline their child?

Where does this leave a parent wanting to follow their God-given responsibility to discipline their child? If there are no consequences for poor actions, then why would the child behave? Why would they respect you? Why would or should we expect them to grow up into mature, honest, respectable adults?

With this kind of enforcement to be "politically correct," it's no wonder that some parents have forgotten the Biblical teachings on discipline. Let's stop and take a look at one of them.

> Proverbs 13:24 says, "Whoever spares the rod hates his son, but he who loves him is diligent to discipline him."

That's a pretty clean and clear verse that says if we love our children, we will discipline them. How many parents do you know that discipline their kids?

I remember my dad telling me that when he would get in trouble at school, he would be disciplined at home. His parents and teachers took a very active role in his upbringing and discipline.

Whatever happened to those days? Why can't there be discipline in the schools? Or at home? When there was discipline like that, you didn't hear of kids blowing up or shooting schools or even killing their parents in their sleep. That kind of behavior just didn't happen when tough love and discipline were present in children's lives.

In Ephesians chapter 6 we see that just because parents can and should discipline, they should be careful. Let's take a look at it for a second.

> Ephesians 6:1-4 says, "Children, obey your parents in the Lord, for this is right. "Honor your father and mother" (this is the first commandment with a promise), "that it may go well with you and that you may live long in the land." Fathers, do not provoke your children to anger, but bring them up in the discipline and instruction of the Lord."

Generally, the temptation is to stop at the first part of verse 2 that says "children obey your parents," and we do not pay attention to the rest of the passage.

Mainly because we get so wrapped up in shoving that verse in our child's face saying, "See, look at that, booyah! You have to obey me, kid!"[21]

However, we see that there is some work to be done on the parental side as well. I like the New King James version of verse 4 when it says, "Fathers, do not provoke your children to wrath…" I want to take a second and break down that part of the verse, "Do not provoke to wrath."

This passage says, "Do not provoke." What does it mean to provoke? In the original Greek, it can mean to stimulate a reaction, deliberately annoy, or incite anger in someone. It means that parents should not place unreasonable blame on a child, give annoying, distressing commands, or harass them. This can discourage children and cause them mental and spiritual harm. We are to be fair, stern, and able to train; behaving like our Heavenly Father.

Imagine a parent wanting to train their child to have a servant's heart and attitude. A parent asks the child for a glass of water, as the child gets the water, the parent wants it in a bigger glass. The child brings a bigger glass, now the parent wants 2.34 ice cubes in the glass. After carefully measuring whatever 2.34 ice cubes is, the parent now wants a slice of lemon no more than 4.68 centimeters thick in the glass.

---

[21] Who says booyah anymore?

Finally the child, after a half hour of trying to get this all accomplished, the parent says, "Never mind, I want a glass of milk."

Would that not be frustrating and cause you to get angry? Imagine you being that child and your favorite TV show was on that you had been waiting for all week, or your friends wanted you to play outside but had gone home since you took too long getting water? How mad would you be? How effective was that exercise in training and teaching? Was it helpful or did it just cause unnecessary anger and provoke unhealthy emotions?

As we look at the rest of the verse, it says to train and instruct. This can often be very time consuming and is always more difficult. Often this process comes with a form of failure and corrective action. Patience is what's needed and required. We want children to honor, but we don't want to do the work required for it.

Men, I want take a moment and point out that we as fathers are to take the leadership role and raise our children. We cannot let others do it, and there have been numerous studies conducted that show the impact a father can have on their sons and daughters.[22]

---

[22] A great resource to read and learn more about being a godly man, husband, and father would be Point Man by Steve Farrar.

Another passage that I think would be good to look at is Hebrews 12:7-11 which says,

> It is for discipline that you have to endure. God is treating you as sons. For what son is there whom his father does not discipline? If you are left without discipline, in which all have participated, then you are illegitimate children and not sons. Besides this, we have had earthly fathers who disciplined us and we respected them. Shall we not much more be subject to the Father of spirits and live? For they disciplined us for a short time as it seemed best to them, but he disciplines us for our good, that we may share his holiness. For the moment all discipline seems painful rather than pleasant, but later it yields the peaceful fruit of righteousness to those who have been trained by it.

God loves us so much that He is willing to discipline us, and if He, with all of His love and compassion, can discipline us as His children, then shouldn't we follow His example? Or should we just ignore this passage for the sake of being politically correct?

I have noticed a trend that has vastly been becoming popular in today's society. This trend is where the parent becomes the child's best friend and not the parent.[23]

---

[23] I call this trend 'parental friend-itis'

I see moms and dads dressing like they are seventeen again, trying to act hip, and trying to fit in with a crowd that is 20 years younger.

Parents, even grandparents, walking around with their pants sagging, their "tighty-whities" showing, even trying to figure out how to use the current slang and lingo. They try to fit into a miniskirt that is two sizes too small and have at least a pound of make-up on to try and look young.[24]

You can tell them apart from the younger generation because they are the ones struggling with the latest technology.[25]

I believe the old adage applies, "Spare the rod, spoil the child." Don't be the friend, be the parent. I know it is not as fun, but we have a responsibility to raise our children. We have to answer to God for how we raise and influence the next generation of believers.

---

[24] Sometimes the makeup is so thick and covered it looks like they applied their makeup with a paint ball gun. Ladies, please do not apply makeup like this; you are naturally beautiful. A little make-up is not bad, but you are beautiful the way God made you.

[25] Seriously, a digital camera does not take film, and we will not go back to a rotary style phone, so get used to a touch screen.

You are the older person, and sorry to say, but no matter how much makeup or how cool you dress, you will be the elder. So to quote a famous singer, "Act your age, not your shoe size."[26]

For you fathers out there afraid of disciplining your children, read and memorize Hebrews 12:9-11. God has put discipline in our lives so that we can grow and have peace. It is not fun to discipline or to be disciplined, but it is essential in the life of every human being.

This passage in Hebrews is encouraging because we know that we are disciplined for our good. If God disciplines us for our good, then we, as we strive to be more like God, should discipline our children as well. But what happens if we fail to discipline?

Let's look at a passage of scripture that shows what happens when you don't give your children the discipline that they need. It is a long passage, but I think it is worth reading and taking the time to see how parenting can go wrong without discipline.

Please take a moment and read 1 Samuel, chapter 2.

---

[26] Prince, for those who do not know.

Did you read that? The Bible called these boys *scoundrels*. This is serious! It is not just that they were bad, but to describe them as scoundrels went a step further. Scoundrels implies that they were good for nothing, unscrupulous, and dishonest.

Eli's sons were nothing but lying, cheating, adulterous people who were using their position for their own gain by manipulation and heresy. In essence, they were taking not only from the people, but from God, as if He wouldn't know.

It also says that their sin was great in the sight of the Lord. How scary is that? God is saying that He saw their sin as a great sin against Him. Not just any sin, a great sin.

We can see from this example that Eli knew what his sons were doing, and although he spoke to them about it, he really didn't do a lot. Eli did not take the corrective action needed to ensure that his home was in order. Fathers, as the head of the household, it is your responsibility to ensure that those in the home are obeying the Lord and all that He commands.

Eli was being politically correct, not wanting people to find out about what was going on and trying to ignore the problem hoping it would all go away. Going back to our illustration at the beginning, Eli was allowing his sons to try and juggle loaded handguns. As a result, not only did they come into judgment, but Eli did as well.

How many parents do you know that ignore or downplay their child's inappropriate behavior instead of disciplining their children? Don't get me wrong, I think that it is very important to talk with your children about everything, but there is a time and place.

Today's society wants parents to talk and nothing else, but talk and if talking can't fix the problem, then it can't be fixed. Look at the afternoon talk shows, they are great examples of how our secular society thinks and wants you to behave with your children, but God has other plans in mind.

Eli's sons sinned and misbehaved so badly that we see in verse 25 and 34 that the Lord wanted to kill them.[27] Although it isn't stated in the Bible, I often think that had Eli done a better job of parenting his sons, they might not have provoked God's wrath.

I also wonder how much of it was Eli's fault and how much of it was the fact that Satan had a better grip on his two son's lives. At times, a parent can do everything right and do everything in their power to help and teach their kids, but their children still get off course and stray from the path. In these cases, the only thing we can do is drop to our knees and pray.

---

[27] I am not going to lie, that is pretty bad when God wants to kill you.

Parents, the only thing we can do is everything we can do. Once we release them from our care, we then place them in God's care. Do not underestimate the power of prayer. If you have children who are straying, give it to God, and trust that He can make it right. Keep fighting the fight, it *is* worth it!

Discipline and respect all start with family time. In our culture we are subject to these weird and demented visions of what family time is. TV shows such as *Married with Children*, *The Simpsons*, *Family Guy,* and a host of others, all point to and insinuate that this is how life should be. Dad gets home, opens a beer and watches TV while the mother attempts to control the house by doing everything for the family; meanwhile the kids are running around getting into trouble.

We watch these shows and laugh, and they are intended for our entertainment, but how often do we catch ourselves saying or thinking "Oh, we are not like that" or "They did it, why can't I?" The best one is "Yeah. I work hard just like that, and I deserve to relax like that." Guys, contrary to popular belief, your job or work place is not your primary responsibility. Yes, you might work there and get a paycheck to provide for your family, but the real work starts when you get home.

According to The Bureau of Labor Statistics, the average American household watches between 2.8 hours and 4.6

hours of television in a 24 hour period.[28] This is just for working adults -- it goes up even more when not working. That is a lot of time watching TV.

Imagine that you sleep for eight hours and work for eight, now you are at 16 hours of the 24 hours that you have in a day. For the sake of argument, let's say that you eat for 3 hours a day, 1 hour per meal, so you are at 19 hours out of a 24 hour day. That leaves you with 5 hours left. Oh wait, what about travel time and chores? Or the "honey-do list"? When you start figuring and crunching the numbers, it is easy to see why so many homes, families and children fall apart.

Lack of discipline, as stated before, is a major part of parenting. But almost as great, is the need for interaction and being a role model for our next generation. I want to talk to dads for a moment because scripture states that fathers are to be the head of the home[29].

A familiar temptation that many fathers face when they get home is to think that they need to "relax." So they do just that, leaving their wives to do the work around the house, including the cooking, cleaning, the discipline, and raising of the children.

---

[28] U.S. Department of Labor, Bureau of Labor Statistics, *American Time Use Survey, 2014 Results* (Washington, DC: June 24, 2015), http://www.bls.gov/news.release/pdf/atus.pdf, 2.
[29] Ephesians chapter 5

Relaxing is not bad, but too much of a good thing can have adverse effects. What kind of message would spending too much time "relaxing" send to your kids? Could it look something like this? "My dad doesn't have to help, why should I?" Or maybe the thought, "He is more interested in his TV than me, so why should I care or even try?"

Fathers reading this, don't fool yourself into thinking that your kids are not watching every move that you make. Every time you tell them to leave you alone, yell at your wife, ignore them for your own personal interests/hobbies, or let them get away with something, they notice. It sticks in their young impressionable minds, leaving warped views on morals, values, and biblical perspectives.

We will speak more on this topic in a different chapter. Right now I want to focus on family time and how you use it.

Stop for a moment and think about when the last time was that you had a family night. What did you do? Did you talk? Did you play a game? Or did you do like most American families, sit down to a huge pizza and watch TV or a movie for three hours and call that family time?

What on earth would we do if we didn't have technology to entertain us? The TV, the cell phone, the computer, video games, and a whole host of other media and devices that entertain and are designed to help us pass the time.

Stop and think of the last time your family got together

and played a board game, cards, or just sat and hung out together, catching up on school, work or life in general? What people often do not realize is that some of the best memories in life are the ones that do not cost much or that are not planned.

There was a family who had two children, a daughter and son. They all had really nice things and drove very nice cars, went on extravagant vacations and had several houses. From the outside, everything seemed to be going perfect for this family. Looking closer at the family, a person could easily start to tell that something did not add up.

The children were unhappy and the parents felt alone and distant. Both parents worked full-time jobs, 50-60 hours a week, just to support the habits and lifestyle that they had become accustomed to before they had been married and had children.

One day, their children expressed their wish for their parents to spend time with them. The daughter wanted her mom to teach her how to cook, sew, talk, and hang out. The son wanted his dad to teach him to fish, and change the oil in his car, and other father/ son activities. The unfortunate part of this was that every time the kids wanted to do some of these things, they would get pushed aside with the saying, "I don't have time. I'm busy. Maybe later."

These parents worked so hard to provide fun things that they thought their children wanted, but neglected to give them what they needed. They got so caught up in their lives that they didn't make time to enjoy their lives and live as a family.

Before you start patting yourself on the back, maybe step back a second and look at your life. You or your family may not fit in this extreme example just given, but what are some areas that may take priority or that can hinder you from your family? Take a second and pray, asking God to help highlight some areas in your life that may need some work so that you can better serve Him and love your family.

As we move on, I would like to point out that there is something to be said about providing for your family and household. A Christian does his or her best to use what God has given them to stay out of debt and provide. We will be talking about this in more depth in a later chapter.

I would like to share a quote with you from Dr. James Dobson that says,

> "What is the biggest obstacle facing the family right now? It is over-commitment; time pressure. There is nothing that will destroy family life more insidiously than hectic schedules and busy lives, where spouses are too exhausted to communicate, too worn out to have sex, too fatigued to talk to the kids. That frantic lifestyle is

just as destructive as one involving out-broken sin. If Satan can't make you sin, he'll make you busy, and that's just about the same thing."[30]

Take a moment and let that sink in. What does your home life look like? Are you striving to have a godly home or a home that resembles television shows and modern, secular culture? Is it a Christ-based or a Christ-less home life? What does scripture say?

> Psalm 127:3-5 says, "Behold, children are a heritage from the Lord, the fruit of the womb a reward. Like arrows in the hand of a warrior are the children of one's youth. Blessed is the man who fills his quiver with them! He shall not be put to shame when he speaks with his enemies in the gate."

> Romans 8:16-17 says, "The Spirit himself bears witness with our spirit that we are children of God, and if children, then heirs—heirs of God and fellow heirs with Christ, provided we suffer with him in order that we may also be glorified with him."

> 1 Timothy 5:8 says, "But if anyone does not provide for his relatives, and especially for members of his household, he has denied the faith and is worse than an unbeliever."

---

[30] James Dobson. AZQuotes.com

These are just a few verses, but they touch on the subject of family in our lives. There are a couple of things I would like to point out very quickly from these verses, but I encourage you and your family to sit down and dig deeper.

First, children are blessings, not burdens. They are gifts from God. Secondly, we are all in the family of God. We should follow God's example of leading a family and incorporate it into our own family life. Finally, we are to provide for our families, not just be a burden on them.

These points may seem like "duh" moments, but sometimes we miss the "duh" moments in a verse because we either skim over them or just ignore them all together. Sometimes we all need to be reminded of even the simplest commands and examples so that we can, as a family of God, raise our own families the way God would have it, not as society would have it.

I am reminded of something that I found in a house once. I was helping a gentleman in our church with a remodeling project on a home that he had purchased. This house, prior to him purchasing it, had belonged to a drug user and drug dealer. As we went through the house, it became apparent to me that the drug-using family had children. By the amount of stuffed animals left behind in one of the bedrooms, I guessed that they had young children.

As we went into the master bathroom to start cleaning from the mess that the previous owner had left, I found an unopened note behind the toilet simply addressed "Daddy." I opened the letter and a child's writing said, "Oakland Raiders rock. Love you… Robin"

This child had left a note to their dad trying to encourage and bond with him. Instead of taking time to read it, the dad carelessly tossed it aside, probably towards a garbage can, and it was left behind the toilet, never read.

I still have this note to this day because it reminds me of how cruel and uncaring some people can be towards their children. I don't care how busy you seem to think your life is; take time and make time for your children. Who knows what little letter or moment you could be missing out on.

> God doesn't measure success in fatherhood by the world's standards. Our daughters are so inherently precious in His sight that our effectiveness as Dads will be proved by the unwavering plumb lines of their lives…[31]

---

[31]Michael Farris, What *a Daughter Needs From Her Dad*. 2004 Bethany House Publishers, Bloomington, MN.

I would like to take that thought and expand on it. If parents realized that they are measured by their children and not by their job or how much money they made or where they went, how much better would the parenting be?

I shudder to think of how many parents reading this book have at one time or another neglected the responsibility of being a parent, or perhaps they forget that they have to answer to God for the children He has blessed them with.

Please do not misunderstand me, Parenting is difficult and there is not an easy way about it. Mistakes will be made and there will be times when we can do nothing but cry out to Jesus for help. That's okay, God is there to help us, and so is God's family. We, as believers, are all here to help each other out, even if it is as simple as babysitting for a night so that the parents can get away for a few hours.

How did your parents raise you? Did they follow God and His laws? Or did they do what everyone else did? Did they use the television as their guide? Did they compare their parenting to other parents, instead of what God would want? There are a ton of bad parenting examples in the world today.

How do I know this? Look at the news! Children blowing up schools, killing people, the increased robbery rate, the suicides, the increase of depression, youth pregnancy on the rise, and the list goes on and on.

We as Christians are not to hide or blend in to this world; we are to stand out proclaiming God's goodness and glory for the world to see.

Parents, you are on the front line, raising the next generation to continue serving God and to have a love for Him that everyone can see.

Please do not give in to the pressures preached by society, and do not give in to being politically correct in your home.

We as believers must be more concerned with being biblically correct than politically correct in the upbringing of our children.

We as believers are not to camouflage the Gospel of Christ, but to make sure the whole world can see it. Where is the starting place? The starting place is with our families and in our homes.

Playing off an old cliché goes something like this: If home is where the heart is, and your heart belongs to God, then shouldn't God be our home? If God is our home, then shouldn't God be in our home while we are here on earth?

If God is at the center of our home and not just an afterthought when we are moving the Bible in order to dust our bookshelf or coffee table, how would that change our lives in our home?

How would that change the way we raise our children? How would that change our behavior? How could that change the world God has placed us in?

I would like to end with a few quotes about family that will hopefully encourage and help along the way.

James C. Dobson- "It is my view that our society can be no more stable than the foundation of individual family units upon which it rests. Our government, our institutions, our schools… indeed, our ways of life are dependent on healthy marriages and loyalty to the vulnerable little children around our feet."

Charles Swindoll – "A family is a place where principles are hammered and honed on the anvil of everyday living."

D.L. Moody – "A man ought to live so that everybody knows he is a Christian… and most of all, his family ought to know."

Discussion Questions

- What are some steps right now that you can take to have a healthier and happier family?
- What are some areas that you can improve on to incorporate God into your home?
- What is one takeaway from this chapter that you can start practicing right now?

Mark Taylor

2

THE POLITICALLY CORRECT CHRISTIAN AND THE GOVERNMENT

"The Government, what are you talking about? Haven't you heard of separation of Church and State? I think that you're crazy, Mark. This chapter doesn't need to be in the book." For those of you who are thinking along this line, just be patient and keep reading.

Without getting ahead of ourselves, we must take time to understand what our role is in our government as Christians. God, in His infinite wisdom, placed us in this location, in this time with these circumstances. We, as believers, must strive to see what He would want us to do and how to use our position and freedom to further the Kingdom of God.

One example of how a Christian should act in regards to the government is found in Daniel chapter 3. In this chapter, King Nebuchadnezzar has made an image to be worshiped, and at the appointed time everyone would worship the image. Three men, Shadrach, Meshach, and Abednego stood up against the king and his rule because it went against what God wanted.

These three men stood against that form of government and stood up for God and His rule. This account took place a long time ago, around 2nd Century B.C. However, I believe that their examples are timeless and can be used to help us, as Christians, live and witness in today's society within our government. Please take a moment to read Daniel chapter 3.

As we work through this chapter, think about how Daniel chapter 3 relates to our government. In verse 1, it reads that "King Nebuchadnezzar made an image of gold…" He thought that he was more important and more powerful than God and tried to show it by making a statue of gold.

Although there are still beliefs and areas in the world that have idol worship, in America this is not the norm. Most Americans do not have an idol of gold in their homes; they do not sacrifice live chickens or perform other weird practices. However, the problem of idols and/or practices do exist that can easily take the place of God in our lives.

I remember when President Obama was first elected to office, and the next few weeks there were all sorts of offers and options to commemorate the "momentous occasion." One such advertisement that caught my attention was the offer to purchase a limited edition, pure gold coin with Obama's face on it.

Before I go any further, I want to say that there is nothing wrong with collecting coins, unless they become your idol and cause a break in your relationship with God.

Having said that, I would also like to point out that after President Obama was elected, people spent thousands of dollars on memorabilia in celebration of the occasion and of the man. Yet how do Americans celebrate the birth and resurrection of Jesus Christ who, being perfect, paid the sacrifice so that we could be with Him? With cheap plastic Easter eggs and of a fat man dressed in red during the month of December.

No matter who a person is -- president, millionaire, pastor, boss, doctor, or whoever -- they are all imperfect and flawed humans not worthy of praise. Only God, being the essence and standard of perfection, deserves our worship.

We move on to verses 4 and 5. Daniel chapter 3 says,

> And the herald proclaimed aloud, "You are commanded, O peoples, nations, and languages, that when you hear the sound of the horn, pipe, lyre, trigon, harp, bagpipe, and every kind of music, you are to fall down and worship the golden image that King Nebuchadnezzar has set up."

Not only did King Nebuchadnezzar think so highly of himself that he built a statue of himself, he went one step further and made everyone worship it. When we think of worship, we generally think of bowing down or singing praise songs, but there are many other forms of worship that we not even realize we participate in. Sometimes we, as believers, can offer worship to things other than God and not even realize it. Let's take a quick moment to look at a few.

Time: Often we devote massive amounts of time to the things that are the most important to us. Devoting time to something is an act of worship. Pause for a second and ask yourself, what kind of things do you spend the most time on? Could it be your job, family, pleasure, social media, fishing, hunting, gossiping with your closest friends? What is it in your life that consumes you and your thoughts? What do you focus your time on in life? Is it God and what He wants, or is it you and your wants?

How can we tell the difference between selfish wants and following what God wants? A great way to know is by running our actions and time management through God's filter called the Bible. We, as believers, should strive to search God's Word for how He would want us to spend our time that He has given us on this earth. To have good time management is important so that we can balance the responsibilities of what God has called us to do. Time management is not only holy, but healthy.

When it comes to time, there can be extremes on both sides of the issue -- from working constantly till death, to the extreme opposite of a person who never works a day in their life. A good balance is what God wants. That's why, even though He did not need to rest, He took a Sabbath to set an example.

Numerous research evidences and findings have shown that if a person is a workaholic, there will be a higher chance of stress and stress-related health issues. Burnout, nervous breakdown, stroke and heart attack are just a few of these health issues.

I am not saying that we should always relax or be lazy. I am also not saying that we should just work ourselves to death. What I believe the Bible says is that we only have a short time on earth, and we should use the time God has given us wisely. We are to serve Him and worship Him, not ourselves or our possessions.

> Philippians 4:8 says, "Finally, brothers, whatever is true, whatever is honorable, whatever is just, whatever is pure, whatever is lovely, whatever is commendable, if there is any excellence, if there is anything worthy of praise, think about these things."

When we put so much effort thinking and planning on our own selfish desires for our lives, we often do not leave any room for God. How can we worship God and follow after Him if we are always consumed with our own thoughts?

Please be careful, as we are all guilty of this at one time or another. My hope is that we can all grow and become more aware of our thought life and, consequently, our time management so that we can be used effectively by God and for God.

Priorities: We often prioritize our lives in matter of importance. Prioritizing can be an indicator of what we worship. The most important things in our lives are what consumes us and our thought life; sports, family, school, relationships, jobs, relaxing, drinking, partying, being perfect, cooking, and the list could go on. You see, whether we realize it or not, when we place things in our lives as being more important than God, we are worshiping those other things.

I like how Kyle Idleman states it in his book, *God's at War*. He says, "What you are searching for and chasing after reveals the god that is winning the war on your heart… your heart defines and determines who you are, how you think, what you do."[32]

Kyle also references Proverbs 4:23 that says, "Keep your heart with all vigilance, for from it flow the springs of life." The point being that what we prioritize in our lives is a great indicator of where our hearts are and what we are valuing and worshiping in our lives.

---

[32] Kyle Idleman, *God's at War: Defeating the Idols That Battle for Your Heart*. Grand Rapids, MI: Zondervan, 2013.

What are some others ways that you are tempted to worship something other than God? Does the feeling of acceptance rule how you worship? Pause for a moment and really take an honest evaluation of your worship life. Pray that God will illuminate areas that can be changed for Him. Let's go back to our passage in Daniel.

In verse 6 of Daniel chapter 3, we see that there was a punishment for not following the law. Verse 6 says, "And whoever does not fall down and worship shall immediately be cast into a burning fiery furnace."

How often are there punishments for not obeying the laws in our government? No matter how dumb the law may be, if we don't follow it, we can be disciplined for it. Maybe not being literally tossed in a fiery furnace, but we can be punished.

Often times when the government or a certain group of people do not like something, they start out by saying that it is politically incorrect.[33] Then if that doesn't work, they start trying to pass laws and rules in order to enforce their own personal beliefs and agenda.

---

[33] This tactic is used often, not just by a group but by individuals as well. It is intended to promote a feeling of guilt and cause pressure to conform, because really, who doesn't want to be considered a good person, to be correct, to be liked? Can anyone say peer pressure?

They preach tolerance for all, yet they are intolerant of others' beliefs and faith, more often they are intolerant of the Christian beliefs and faith. Weird, right?

When I was in college, there was a certain group on campus that were very active in expressing their social/political views. This group was extremely quick to complain about views or opinions counter to theirs. One day, on the urging of this particular group, the school came up with "Safe Zones." These "Safe Zones" were marked with a sticker and/or plaque on the wall where people couldn't talk about their own views if it could offend someone.

The problem was that these stickers and plaques were plastered all over the campus, and it was all in an attempt to control what people could say. Although, right beside one of these "Safe Zone" stickers was a student's photo exhibit where there were graphic nude pictures of his male partner.

I will never understand how they justified that. I couldn't say what I thought was right or wrong, but things that would offend me and/or are illegal for minors to see were allowed to be hung on the walls at the school. All was done in the name of art and in the name acceptance and tolerance.

How many other schools and college campuses across this nation are imposing this kind of political correctness? What kind of punishment or discipline are they using to enforce this kind of behavior?

How can a place of education be so discriminatory and narrow-minded as to say that one cannot have the Ten Commandments on the wall, but graphic pictures and other offensive materials are fine?

With this kind of double standard in places like schools, work, community centers, and our government, there is a question that must be asked. Are you willing to offend in order to share the Gospel? How far would you go to follow God's Great Commission?

> Matthew 28:18-20 says, "And Jesus came and said to them, All authority in heaven and on earth has been given to me. Go therefore and make disciples of all nations, baptizing them in the name of the Father and of the Son and of the Holy Spirit, teaching them to observe all that I have commanded you. And behold, I am with you always, to the end of the age."

As we move onto verse 7 of Daniel chapter 3, it states that "all the peoples, nations and men of every language fell down and worshiped the image of gold…"

Remember when we were kids, we would get into trouble and our excuse to our parents was, "Well, everyone else is doing it!" And without missing a beat, their response was, "Well, if everyone jumped off a bridge, would you?"

How often are we enticed by peer pressure? We find ourselves doing, saying, and thinking things because everyone else around us is thinking and doing those things.

Reflecting back for a moment on your youth, were there times that you gave into peer pressure? How did you feel? Were you accepted because you joined in and gave into peer pressure?

This is cliché, but if everyone else did actually jump off a bridge, would you? No! Then why is it that so many people, including Christians, find themselves doing things that compromise their integrity, morality, ethics, and spiritual well-being for the sake of conforming and acceptance?

Look at recent history. Well-known and well-educated Christians that people look up to and admire fall almost every day. Sadly, the news is full of stories of how pastors, priests, and religious leaders were convicted of rape, drugs, cheating, stealing from the church, and participating in homosexual activities.

These Christian authors, leaders, pastors, and mentors who thought they would never get caught, are being drug down and run through the muck and mire of our world. Sadly they are taking the name of Jesus Christ with them through the turmoil. Did they give in to peer pressure? Did they conform to this world? Did they feel more accepted by giving in to such temptation?

Please take a moment and pray for those who are leaders in your local church and around your city. Pray for them to receive wisdom, strength, and insight to navigate through life and to be protected from the devil's traps and snares.

The most common responses from people who have fallen are, "Well, other people were doing it, so I thought it wouldn't be that big of a deal," or "It's not illegal. The government says it's okay, so why can't I do it?" A word of caution to those who are reading this and are in a leadership position or are aspiring to be in a leadership position.

> James 3:1 says, "Not many of you should become teachers, my brothers, for you know that we who teach will be judged with greater strictness."

How do you think that this kind of behavior happened to these "giants of the faith"? Why did they start to waiver on their beliefs? Did it just happen? Was it a surprise? Most of the time these things happen slowly and it creeps up on people because we are not careful to guard our hearts and/or we start to compromise. Once we start compromising our beliefs, values, and ethics, where does it stop? I mean, if you can compromise on one issue, then why not others?

This is where political correctness creeps into play. *Just give in a little, it won't hurt anyone. There will be no damage done, and just be accepting.* Our thoughts and behaviors start to conform to this world, and our actions, or lack thereof, start to have a heavy impact on who we are.

Once we start letting this kind of thought process and behavior become the accepted norm, then the government steps into our lives, knowing what's best for us, and starts passing laws to ensure that we do what is politically correct: All in the name of fairness, political correctness, tolerance and acceptance so we don't hurt anyone's feelings. Next thing you know it will be a crime in this country to be a Christian.

How often do we, as Christians, allow the government to walk over us as a church, establishing rules and regulations all in the name of peace and harmony? How does peer pressure shape us and make us compromise and conform to the majority? We allow the government, and others not of the faith, to influence us and walk on the church as if we were a door mat with a cross on it.

We allow the mishaps of our religious leaders to define who we are as a group. We put up with their behavior and allow the outside world to judge us and form opinions about us by their actions. This allows for them to use these opinions and general assumptions about Christians to place more pressure on us as a body of believers to conform to what they would want, not what God would want.

For example, one day I was speaking with a person at the retail store I was working at during my college years. The person asked what I was going to school for. I replied that I was studying to be a pastor, to which he replied, "Oh, well, don't be playing with boys like them others do."

He was implying that, because of the actions of a few priests in the Catholic Church, that all religious leaders were like that and formed his opinion based on that information. I informed him that there was a huge difference and that he couldn't make a general assumption based on the actions of a few.

Because believers fail to stand for what they know is right, they fail and fall into the temptation to give in. They have no courage, no conviction, no command of their faith and beliefs. Again, going back to our passage in Daniel, let's look at how these three men handled their opposition.

Verse 8 of Daniel chapter 3 says, "Therefore at that time certain Chaldeans came forward and maliciously accused the Jews." And verse 12 says, "There are certain Jews whom you have appointed over the affairs of the province of Babylon: Shadrach, Meshach, and Abednego. These men, O king, pay no attention to you; they do not serve your God's or worship the golden image that you have set up."

Now we are at what I call the meat and potatoes of the passage. These three men stood for what they believed in, even in the face of trouble. How amazing would it be if we, as Christians, would have even just a little of that courage to stand firm no matter the cost?

The funny thing is that we can have that courage, not to go lose our job or go around looking for ways to upset people or be persecuted, but when the time comes to follow Christ, we can have the confidence and courage to do so. A simple verse that most of us are familiar with is found in Philippians 4:13, "I can do all things through Christ who strengthens me."

When our faith is found in Christ, when we are giving our all and we feel like there is nothing else to give, we can take rest in knowing that Christ will give us strength. There is nothing in this life that we cannot overcome for the furthering of God's Kingdom. Like the three men in the book of Daniel, God is with us even when we feel alone. We as believers are never alone.

Let's continue on in Daniel. Don't you just love the tattle tale? You know who I am talking about, that one person that always rats you out for things? In Daniel 3:12, that is what happened to Shadrach, Meshach, and Abednego. These Chaldeans were not liking these three Jewish men, and when they found an opportunity to rat them out, they did. I cannot count how many times I have witnessed the actions of a few that ruin the lives of many.

I am reminded of a news story that I heard about a few years ago. This story took place in a local high school in Louisiana. During the graduation ceremony, there was going to be a prayer, as was the custom of this school, and so many other schools around the country during these kinds of ceremonies. However, because of an atheist high school student, the school had to cancel its prayer because of this one student.

The school didn't care about the other graduating students that didn't mind the prayer or actually wanted the prayer in the commencement. They let the actions of one determine the results for many. The student went so far as to say that he didn't even want God mentioned in the ceremony.

As a side note, I find it very funny that an atheist would get so upset about a prayer to a God that they don't even believe exists. How would they say the Pledge of Allegiance? "One nation under the sky, indivisible…" or would they just not say the Pledge of Allegiance because it mentions someone they believe doesn't exist?

I am still confused as to how one single person could change how things were done at this school. The question arises, that if there were even five Christian students that took a stand, would they have removed the prayer?

I wonder if they would have been afraid or just didn't care about it. If one person can change an entire school ceremony, what could two or three students on fire for God accomplish?

As we can see from this passage in Daniel, Shadrach, Meshach and Abednego knew what would happen, but they chose to stand up for what they knew was right. These three men give a great example that nothing is as important in this world than standing up for God and for what you believe in.

In the verses that follow, they bring Shadrach, Meshach, and Abednego before King Nebuchadnezzar and he is furious. So he asks them the question in verse 15, "…Who is the god who will deliver you out of my hands?"

Let's break in and see what Shadrach, Meshach, and Abednego's response was in Daniel 3:16-18.

> Shadrach, Meshach, and Abednego answered and said to the king, "O Nebuchadnezzar, we have no need to answer you in this matter. If this be so, our God whom we serve is able to deliver us from the burning fiery furnace, and he will deliver us out of your hand, O king. But if not, be it known to you, O king, that we will not serve your God's or worship the golden image that you have set up.

Wow! Talk about conviction and courage in the face of the government and persecution. If you think that they didn't know what they were in for, then take a moment and read this passage again. They knew full well what was going to happen to them if they stood up to the king and his rule.

In the days of Daniel, they didn't have a government like we have today. Can you imagine going before the ruler of the land, the guy in charge, and telling him, "You don't impress me, I don't answer to you, and no matter what you try to do to me, know that my God is more powerful than you will ever be, so do your worst." That would be something. What faith, what courage, what an amazing example of how we as Christians should live! God is our master, God is our ruler, God is our King!

In today's society we don't even have huge burning furnaces to be thrown in, the worst is jail. Yet somehow we are more afraid of hurting people's feelings than letting the government control our lives by instilling upon us their moral, ethical, and spiritual values. We are more afraid of that than we are of answering to God, the only God, the one who gives us our very breath.

Are there some examples in your life that illustrate this point? Are there people over you, over your family, over your life that impact how you live, or impact what you are to allow and/or be accepting of? Are there instances that cause you to sacrifice your convictions for the sake of being politically correct?

In April of 2009, the Iowa Supreme Court stated that it was legal for homosexuals to be married[34] and proceeded to make the county recorders follow through with their ruling.[35] In essence, the Court was forcing the recorders to break the law by allowing homosexuals to get married. The courts created a law because there was no law in Iowa stating that men could marry men or women could marry women.[36]

The bigger issue that came up was the question, what if homosexual couples wanted to get married in a church? Would the government make the pastor marry them? If the church refused, would the pastor go to jail? I remember a few scary weeks where we were not sure what was going to happen.

I remember my pastor at that church in Iowa saying that he would be very grateful if someone would post his bail should he be arrested for refusing to conduct such a marriage.

---

[34] Varnum v. Brien. 2009, 07-1499. Iowa District Court. http://www.iowacourts.gov/wfData/files/Varnum/07-1499(1).pdf.
[35] Technically, a court system cannot make or create laws, only interpret what is already spelled out in black and white. They are not to "read between the lines" or get creative with the law, only to say rather the law states one way or another.
[36] For the record, their reason/excuse was that they thought marriage between a man and woman violated the equal protection clause in the Iowa Constitution... I wonder what God thinks the violation is, but that's for another book.

He was concerned that the government would come get him for not being willing to marry a homosexual couple. He was willing to stand up for what God said was correct.

This is a great example of how the government is trying to take over our churches, and trying to control what we say, do, think, act and believe.[37] One of the ways the government could try and control the church would be to threaten the church by taking the tax exemption away if the church didn't do what the government wanted.

Thousands of churches across America are struggling to keep the lights on in the church. If the government took away their exemption status, the church would have to close its doors. Another way is through fines or jail time for those who do not comply.

Sadly, a more recent example has happened in our country. In June of 2015, the Supreme Court ruled 5 to 4 in favor of legalizing the right to same sex marriage for the entire country,.[38] regardless of the fact that states had voted and defined what a marriage was.

What do we do as Christians? Nothing because we wouldn't want to offend anyone? We just want to get along, right? Be politically correct? Let the government and society

---

[37] I know this sounds like a conspiracy theory, but stay with me.
[38] Adam Liptak, "Supreme Court Ruling Makes Same-Sex Marriage a Right Nationwide." *The New York Times*, June 26, 2015. http://www.nytimes.com

warp and change us as children of God so that you couldn't even tell the difference between the children of God and the children of the world?

It should be our prayer every day that we have the courage and strength to stand for what we believe and to obey God's law and His Word, not the words of those around us. We are to love our enemies and to operate in compassion and love. That is not an excuse to be a Christian doormat for the world to wipe their feet on, but to follow Christ and share Christ with the world, no matter the cost.

Discussion Questions

- What are some ways that you, as a believer, could get involved in your local government?
- What, if any, attitudes do you have that might need to be corrected regarding the government?

Mark Taylor

3

THE POLITICALLY CORRECT CHRISTIAN IN THE SCHOOL SYSTEM

"I pledge allegiance to the Flag of the United States of America and to the Republic for which it stands, one Nation under God, indivisible, with liberty and justice for all" We all learned and recited this pledge back in grade school. Focus on the part of the pledge that states "...one Nation under God." Today our educational system and others want to take out the "under God" part because it has now been deemed as being "politically incorrect."

On June 26, 2002, the United States Court of Appeals for the Ninth Circuit in California ruled 2 to 1 that the Pledge of Allegiance violated the First Amendment. Why? Because a parent complained that saying one nation under God had injured his daughter by the assertion that there is a God.[39]

There have been instances where, even in the media, people have omitted the phrase "under God" while reciting

---

[39] This is public record and can be found in numerous places. If you would like to read the transcripts, you can go to your local library or Google it to find the actual legal documents that discuss the ruling, including the appeals that came after the ruling.

the Pledge of Allegiance. In 2011, NBC covered the U.S. Open Championship, and during the Pledge of Allegiance, a person in the editing room decided to trim out the phrase "one nation under God." Although NBC apologized for the action, it shows where we as a society are headed.[40]

Something that I heard as a boy that still sticks with me today was actually from a comedian who took a moment to share a very serious thought about the Pledge of Allegiance. This great comedian's name was Red Skelton, and I would like you to take a moment and read his commentary on the Pledge of Allegiance. Pay close attention to the last part of what he had to say.

> I've been listening to you boys and girls recite the Pledge of Allegiance all semester and it seems as though it is becoming monotonous to you. If I may, may I recite it and try to explain to you the meaning of each word?
>
> I -- me, an individual, a committee of one.
> PLEDGE -- dedicate all of my worldly goods to give without self-pity.
> ALLEGIANCE -- my love and my devotion.
> TO THE FLAG -- our standard, Old Glory, a symbol of freedom. Wherever she waves, there's

---

[40] NBC has had other instances of omitting God from its network according to Fox News. Todd Starnes, "NBC Omits "God" From Pledge of Allegiance...Again." *Fox News*, January 8, 2015. http://www.foxnews.com/opinion

respect because your loyalty has given her a dignity that shouts freedom is everybody's job!

UNITED -- that means that we have all come together.

STATES -- individual communities that have united into 48 great states. Forty-eight individual communities with pride and dignity and purpose; all divided with imaginary boundaries, yet united to a common purpose, and that's love for country.

AND TO THE REPUBLIC -- a state in which sovereign power is invested in representatives chosen by the people to govern. And government is the people and it's from the people to the leaders, not from the leaders to the people.

FOR WHICH IT STANDS, ONE NATION -- one nation, meaning "so blessed by God"

INDIVISIBLE -- incapable of being divided.

WITH LIBERTY -- which is freedom -- the right of power to live one's own life without threats, fear or some sort of retaliation.

AND JUSTICE -- the principle or quality of dealing fairly with others.

FOR ALL -- which means, boys and girls, it's as much your country as it is mine.

And now, boys and girls, let me hear you recite the Pledge of Allegiance:

"I pledge allegiance to the flag of the United States of America, and to the Republic, for which it stands; one nation, indivisible, with liberty and justice for all."
Since I was a small boy, two states have been added to our country and two words have been added to the Pledge of Allegiance...
UNDER GOD
Wouldn't it be a pity if someone said that is a prayer and that would be eliminated from schools too?

I know what you are thinking, "Mark, I thought this book was about God and Christians, not about our Pledge of Allegiance." You would be right, this book isn't about the Pledge of Allegiance, but it is an example of the kind of propaganda that is being taught in our public schools today. It is a measurement of where we are as a society, and what we are becoming. It should be a call to pay close attention to what is going on around us.

Before I move on, I would like to say that as Christians, our allegiance should be to God first. Remember, this world is not our home, we are just passing through. However, I did want to use this example of the Pledge of Allegiance as an illustration of just how far people are willing to go to get their way.

Think about it: if people are willing to try and change the Pledge of Allegiance, the pledge that our entire country has recited for years, what else are they going to try and change?

What else are they going to take over or teach so that they can try to get rid of God altogether?

I remember a while back when the public schools were told that they could not list the Ten Commandments in the building anymore. However, they could list other religious information, such as Muslim belief posters, for the sake of diversity. They took the Ten Commandments away so that other people would not be offended. A question that I have often wondered is why didn't we, as Christians, get offended?

We can and should stand up for what we believe in. We should not let people be so disrespectful of God, our beliefs, faith or one another. We should take a stand against the devil and all that he is trying to do, so that the Gospel can be furthered.

The hardest part is that we are to do it without sin, and we are to be compassionate and loving, not be a pushover or a doormat, but firm, loving, strong individuals for Christ.

Some verses that encourage and address this include:

James 4:7 says, "Submit yourselves therefore to God. Resist the devil, and he will flee from you."

Ephesians 6:10-12 says, "Finally, be strong in the Lord and in the strength of his might. Put on the whole armor of God, that you may be able to stand against the schemes of the devil. For we do not wrestle against flesh and blood, but against the rulers, against the authorities, against the cosmic powers over this present darkness, against the spiritual forces of evil in the heavenly places."

1 Timothy 6:12 says, "Fight the good fight of the faith. Take hold of the eternal life to which you were called and about which you made the good confession in the presence of many witnesses."

We are not to be combative with people, we are to love and share the love of Jesus Christ. However, there does come a time to stand up and be counted for. We are to resist the devil and we are to stand against the schemes of the devil and do what is right for us, for our children, and for God.

Get up, get active, and stop letting society take over and teach our children this line of propaganda and lies. God created this country and He created us. Wake up and start thinking about what God wants and not just what is socially acceptable.

There have been some cases recently that show how parents are getting active in the public school system. These parents are taking a stand and trying to change how their children are being taught and what they are being taught. However, there is a lot of work to do and it will be a long hard journey.

There is a verse that my parents took to heart and I know a lot of other parents took as well when they decided to homeschool their children. It is Proverbs 22:6 that says, "Train up a child in the way he should go; even when he is old he will not depart from it."

As the public education system deteriorates, from teaching the facts to indoctrinating their own personal beliefs and pushing their own agendas, more and more families are homeschooling. In fact, there has been over a 74% increase in homeschooling since 1999.[41]

Before moving on, I would like to mention that it is easy for us to point out flaws in the public school system and turn to the private or homeschool way for a solution. However, if we look closely, even private schools can become pressured into following the politically correct line of thinking.

Private schools either accept what the government wants or they could lose their accreditation, or a host of other punishments. Accreditation has become more of a "good housekeeping" seal of approval for schools from the government. If the school does not teach what the government wants, they just pull the school's accreditation.

Having worked in the public school system and being

---

[41] U.S. Department of Education, National Center for Education Statistics, *The Condition of Education 2009* (Washington, DC: GPO, 2009) http://nces.ed.gov/pubs2009/2009081.pdf, iii.

educated in both the private and homeschool systems, I know what kind of damage can be done. I have had family members in all three forms of education systems, and I can tell you for certain, there are no singular perfect forms of education.

What I do know is that parents need to be involved in their children's education. They need to be active and care about what their children are being taught and what they are learning.[42] It is easier said than done. It takes commitment, time, and sacrifice, but it is completely necessary.

I recently ran into an old friend who had attended the same private school as I had. As we spoke, I soon discovered that he had wandered away from the Lord and wasn't where he should be as a believer in Christ. When he hit college, he lost all self-control and went his own way, forgetting God, the church, and his family.

This kind of incident happens all too frequently. Go to any university, find the "party group," and start talking to them. Some if not a majority will tell you that they had gone to a private school, was homeschooled, or had gone to church as a child, but now they were doing what they wanted.

---

[42] There is a big difference between being taught and learning. Children learn a whole lot more than what they are being taught.

Why is this? After all, they did go to a private school or maybe even homeschooled, right? They went to Sunday school, they sat in church, what could have gone wrong?

More often than not, a child that goes to a private school is often forgotten by the parents spiritually. The parents assume that since their Jonny or Jane goes to a private Christian school that they must be getting their recommended daily dose of God, so they neglect that part of their child's life.

Look at Proverbs 22:6 again. Train -- that means you, as the parent, the one who has the child, or who takes care of them. This does not refer to a school or a friend or even church. Certainly it does not mean the television or Internet. We are to train up a child.

Churches and school systems are there as a help, but ultimately, the responsibility falls to you, the parent, to teach and educate your children. How many problems could have been avoided, how many false teachings never learned, if we would have only taken the time to invest our wisdom into our children.

Parents, please understand that it is not a sin for your children to go to a public school, just be extremely careful what they are learning in and out of the classroom. Some see it more as preparing their kids as missionaries for that school in your community, not just sending them off to learn.

Working in the public school system for a brief time, I have seen some shocking sights. Breaking up fights, sorting out relationships, trying to prevent a suicide in the cafeteria during lunch, and dealing with pregnant seniors, all of which were just a few of the examples that I had to deal with.

One case I remember quite well was that of two brothers. I never understood why they had the behavioral problems that they had until one day I got called over to their house. As I got to the house, I heard yelling and screaming, as if someone were being skinned alive. Entering the house I saw a pair of legs sticking through the ceiling and one of the brothers trying to stab at the legs in the ceiling.

The mother was hysterical not understanding what was going on. As I looked around the house, everything I saw was a disaster with the couch overturned, the front door broken off its hinges, fridge left open with food all over the kitchen. I asked the mom where their father was, and she looked at me and said "That's a good question."

It became apparent to me that some of these issues came back to the parental provision or lack thereof. The mother worked, and when she didn't work, she partied. The father was nonexistent, leaving these two brothers to fend for themselves.

When left to our own means with no one to answer to, we will become, in essence, self-destructive[43], and that was the case with these two boys. They didn't do their homework, clean the house, or do anything productive because they didn't have to. Instead, they would fight, watch TV, drink, smoke, and have other junior high and senior high school girls over... alone.

I tried to witness to them and help out as best as I could, but after a few months, their mom decided to move away, and I have not heard from them since. This happens more than we, as Christians and as human beings, would like to admit. I feel sad that I couldn't help them more, but I do take comfort in knowing that God has a plan and that everything works according to His will.

Far too many parents send their children off to school and let the system raise them. If something goes wrong, they blame anyone and everyone for it, except for themselves. It is time we take a stand and own up to the responsibility of raising our children. I am not saying there's one magical way all parents must raise perfect kids, but I am saying that we need to be active in their lives, especially in their educational lives.

---

[43] Read through the Bible and highlight some passages about sin. No one has to teach us to sin, we come by it naturally. It is embedded in our very nature.

For example, a big topic being discussed in the educational realm is that of evolution vs. creationism. This is a very hot topic because there are even some Christians that believe in evolution, or parts of it. The problem is that it takes as much faith, if not more faith, to believe in evolution as it does in creationism.

Before we move on, I would like to take a second and define some terms so that we are all on the same page.

> **Evolution**: A theory that the various types of animals and plants have their origin in other preexisting types and that the distinguishable differences are due to modifications in successive generations.[44]
>
> **Intelligent Design**: The theory that matter, the various forms of life, and the world were created by a designing intelligence.[45]
>
> **Creationism**: A doctrine or theory holding that matter, the various forms of life, and the world were created by God out of nothing and usually in the way described in Genesis.[46]

---

[44] *Merriam-Webster's Collegiate Dictionary,* s.v. "Evolution."
[45] *Merriam-Webster's Collegiate Dictionary,* s.v. "Intelligent Design."
[46] *Merriam-Webster's Collegiate Dictionary,* s.v. "Creationism."

For the sake of being impartial, I used the Merriam-Webster Dictionary, which is used worldwide for education and teaching. Also, I want to quickly point out that every one of the definitions starts out stating that it is a theory. I am sorry to say this, but to all the scientists and teachers out there stating that evolution is solid fact, it is still a theory.

A theory can be defined as an ideal, a belief, a plausible principle, or an unproved assumption. Based on this definition and the ones above, a teacher cannot say that evolution is a fact and the rest are beliefs. This is only one problem that is brought up when teaching only evolution in the school system.

As seen in the movie *Expelled, No Intelligence Allowed*, Ben Stein points out that if a teacher even mentions intelligent design, not creationism, but intelligent design as a viable option to creation, they can become outcasts in the educational field. With this kind of censorship, propaganda and blatant disregard for fairness in the classroom, it is now more than ever imperative that parents become active in their children's educational lives -- more so for a believer and their family.

What kind of education is that? Only giving one side and not allowing the other sides or viewpoints to even be discussed? What a happy day in the classroom when the teacher says, "Okay, kids today we are going to learn that we came from some sort of sludge, then grew into monkeys and now here you are. Now, no questions because we can't defend or explain things that well, so moving on..."[47]

I thought part of education was about questioning and reasoning what goes on in the world and why. One of the most beautiful things about the Bible is that you can question it, and it will not fail; you can reason against it, and it will always triumph; you can use it for teaching, and it will always give the answers.

> 2 Timothy 3:16 says, "All Scripture is breathed out by God and profitable for teaching, for reproof, for correction, and for training in righteousness."

Another common theme that is becoming very clear as time passes is that Americans are starting to lose their ability to critically think.[48] This does not evade the local church or youth group.

---

[47] I have the utmost respect for teachers in the public and private schools and there are a lot of good ones out there. I am only trying to make a point and do not want you to misunderstand me or miss the point... to be involved in the lives of our children as God has commanded.

[48] If you don't believe me, look it up on the internet, if it is on the internet it must be right, right? Or watch some TV, only the facts are on the TV and we can all trust the media... (insert sarcasm)

The ability to reason or question the information that is being given to them is becoming a lost art. Our students sit in class for eight to nine hours a day five days a week listening to teachers give information and telling them it is correct and to not question it.

As a side note, and in the interest of being fair, take a moment and look at Sunday schools, small groups, youth groups, et cetera. Are they being challenged to wrestle with and contemplate their faith? Or are they being asked to sit and listen as the teacher gives information telling them that it is correct and to not question it?

This is a sobering thought. It is no surprise that we are losing the battle over the minds of the youth. If they are never allowed to question, they never search, and if they never search, they never find answers. The Bible offers all the answers to life's questions and yet, if people do not search, they will not find answers, only questions that they -- teachers, scientists, secular leaders, and the world -- cannot answer.

A lukewarm, politically correct Christian will blend in to the school system. Sure they might be A+ students and never miss a day of class, but are they learning? What are they learning? Are they learning to wrestle with all the information and owning their faith? Are they serving God to their full potential?

Students are in a unique position in that they can reach others in a way that a parent, youth pastor, or the church could never reach. They can impact people in their lives and make a difference that we could only hope to make.

Knowing this, one can quickly see how vital it is to ensure that our youth, junior high, senior high, even college, obtain the correct information and learn to defend what is right.

Having the ability to critically think and logically seek information and be able to reason, wrestle and own their faith is of the utmost importance.

This world is not getting any easier on young people. The public schools and government funded programs are not going to offer the help needed. It is up to the parents, it is up to you to instruct teach and help guide students through life.

We all have a part to play. We can all help and serve and make a change in the educational process. Old, young, single, parents, future parents, youth pastors, everyone can help make a difference, even if it is just by voting on school board issues or by making your opinions known about the school system. We can and must invest in the youth of America and in our churches. If we don't, who will?

We as believers must set and raise the bar, not try to just get under it. We must be leaders as we train and raise up the next generation.

We must be willing to invest and take the risk when no one else is willing. We are commanded to train and instruct.

> 2 Timothy 3:14-17 says, "But as for you, continue in what you have learned and have firmly believed, knowing from whom you learned it and how from childhood you have been acquainted with the sacred writings, which are able to make you wise for salvation through faith in Christ Jesus. All Scripture is breathed out by God and profitable for teaching, for reproof, for correction, and for training in righteousness, that the man of God may be complete, equipped for every good work."

> Proverbs 22:6 says, "Train up a child in the way he should go; even when he is old he will not depart from it"

> Isaiah 54:13 says, "All your children shall be taught by the LORD, and great shall be the peace of your children."

As we go through this life, following after Christ and trying to walk the Christian walk, we must not forget the importance of education. Whether you have children or grandchildren in public school, private school, or even in homeschool, we must take time to get active and involved in the raising of this next generation.

Discussion Questions

- Do you know what your children are being taught?

- Do you know what they are learning?

- Are you in contact with your children even when they are in college to ensure that they are being faithful to God?

- If you are in college, are you remembering and obeying what the Bible says?

- If you do not have any children yet, what steps are you taking to ensure that you will be an active parent in the raising of your children?

- What are some steps that you can take to help raise and teach godly principles in your children and their friends?

4

THE POLITICALLY CORRECT CHRISTIAN IN THE CHURCH

Often times the church is where Christians go to grow, fellowship, be rejuvenated, and worship. Because of this, it is odd that I would include this chapter in the book. The church is assumed to be a safe environment, free from any corrupt behavior, wrong misdoings, or false teachings because, well, it's a church. Because many of us make this assumption, I feel it is important that we take a moment to evaluate the situation and facts.

The church is under attack, not only by the outside world, such as the media and the government, but it is also under attack from itself. It is being attacked by members that are part of the church, both globally and locally. Yes, I said it, the church is under attack by its own body like a deadly cancer.

I know you may be sitting there thinking that I am barking up the wrong tree. For just a moment though I would like you to stop and think, putting aside your own biases and preconceptions, and be willing to take a truthful look at the Body of Christ, better known as the Church.

In America, the church has started to shift from its intended purpose. The church is becoming more of a social club. Instead of worrying about the poor and needy, we worry about what coffee to serve. Instead of providing the Gospel to those near and far, we are providing a comfortable place for Christians to come, hang out, and talk about their next gathering and how much fun it will be.

Churches across America are in danger of losing their zeal for the Lord. They have become more focused on gathering people together and growing their numbers and programs than about preaching and teaching the Word of God. Churches are giving in to the pressure of what they think they should be instead of what they are called to be, which is equipping people to own, practice, and work out their faith in fellowship with one another.

The church is supposed to teach, preach, and help in the spiritual growth of its members, to be a place where people can come to know and experience the love of God. There is a part of the church that is to be a place of fellowship and hanging out, but there is more to it than just that. Fun and games with a good cup of coffee can be good in moderation, but if that becomes the driving force, then we are not being the church God intends for us to be.

Acts 20:28 says, "Pay careful attention to yourselves and to all the flock, in which the Holy Spirit has made you overseers, to care for the church of God, which he obtained with his own blood."

1 Corinthians 10:31-33 says, "So, whether you eat or drink, or whatever you do, do all to the glory of God. Give no offense to Jews or to Greeks or to the church of God, just as I try to please everyone in everything I do, not seeking my own advantage, but that of many, that they may be saved."

Colossians 3:14-16 says, "And above all these put on love, which binds everything together in perfect harmony. And let the peace of Christ rule in your hearts, to which indeed you were called in one body. And be thankful. Let the word of Christ dwell in you richly, teaching and admonishing one another in all wisdom, singing psalms and hymns and spiritual songs, with thankfulness in your hearts to God."

I understand that God will bless a faithful church if they are following God's will. However, when hell is being mentioned less and less in our churches for fear of upsetting the congregation, something is wrong.

When more emphasis is being placed on making everyone that comes to church feel better about themselves, and not seeking to fix and heal the real issues, something is wrong.

There has to be a balance, and sometimes there has to be hurt and pain before we can heal.

There is a growing movement of people -- people in the church, people with influence -- that are becoming more concerned about being politically correct and making the church politically correct than about fulfilling the mission given by God for the church. They in essence, and for the sake of being politically correct, are killing the church. They are also not allowing the body to function as it should.

Reading through 1 Corinthians 12, Paul talks about how the Church is the body of Christ and we are all members of the body. We all have our own jobs, functions, and parts to play. Just because we are not all pastors, does not mean we cannot minister to those around us. The church is here to do the work of God, and each one of us has their part to play and their own job to accomplish for the glory of God.

I want to commend the churches out there that are staying true to the Word of God and are preaching and teaching God's truths for all people. There are many good churches in America and around the world that are not caught up in giving a "great show" or having the "best babysitting service." Rather, they are busy with preaching, teaching, and spreading the message of God with the young and old in any and all ways possible.

My prayer for you is that either you belong to a church like that, or you are helping to make the church even better for the Kingdom of God. Hopefully after reading this chapter you will be able to identify some areas of improvement for your church and God will use you to impact His church for His glory and honor.

I want to direct your attention to the book of Revelation. I want to show you some churches that God was not happy with and why. I want to show you how the members and leaders in these churches came up short and missed what God wanted them to do. In Revelation there are seven churches mentioned in the first few chapters. Encouragement and warning are given to these seven churches.

The Loveless Church, Revelation 2:1-7

At first look, this church is getting major praise from God. They are working, they do not tire, are patient and smart. In today's timeframe, this church would be putting out theologians and authors. A person could walk in there and it would be a smooth operating machine. Yet they are missing one little thing. They have forgotten the love of Christ. God is saying, "Hey, I know you guys are great at working, but you have forgotten Me and My Son, the one who lived a perfect life and died for you."

Today there are a lot of organizations and people groups that love the work of the church, and why wouldn't they? The church helps the needy, the homeless and provides everything they can to better help those who are in need. A politically correct church would do those things and be accepted as a great church by today's standards.

I know you are likely thinking, "What is wrong with that?" My response would be nothing, except that if it is just serving and not sharing the love of Christ, then what is the point? The point is this, there are many organizations that can serve and help the needy and helpless, and to be honest, they do a good job. The church is supposed to do that as well, but also the church is called to share the love and message of Christ.[49]

The church at Ephesus in Revelation 2 had forgotten about their first love, the love of Christ. In our society, this would be a politically correct church and probably pretty well known and loved by society. Why? Because sharing the love of Christ is not accepted in society. It is not okay to preach Christ, of His crucifixion and resurrection, so any institution that can do good while leaving God out is okay by the world's standards.

---

[49] 1 Corinthians 13

Everyone wants and likes the serving aspect of the church because it is free labor and helps those in need, but they do not want the church to share the Gospel message and the Word of God. This shouldn't be surprising since Jesus warned us that His message and its truth would not be accepted. We are still commanded to proclaim it. Sadly, many Christians and churches as a whole are losing their boldness to stand up for Christ and step out of the boat and into the dangerous waters of our society.

Churches serve the poor and needy, they feed the hungry and offer clothing to those who are unclothed. Churches offer teaching programs and service projects for and throughout the community. This and more are all part of a healthy church, but if a church stops there, what will it really accomplish? Our first priority is to witness and show God's love and show Christ as the only way to heaven.

People can see Christ through serving by the way Christians conduct themselves and by how we live. Serving is a great way to give and live a personal testimony. I do not want to belittle that aspect of Christian living; however, there is something to be said about proclaiming Christ's love and sacrifice, offering a verbal testimony of how Christ has changed you and how He is alive and well working in your heart and soul. Even Jesus spoke.

He didn't just live a perfect life and assume that people would understand if He lived well. He spoke, He taught, His actions together with His Words backed it all up.

We as a church and as Christians can accomplish a lot by serving, as it says in James chapter 2, faith without works is dead. We need the working aspect of our faith, but we need to use the opportunities of service to witness, proclaim, and simply talk about the relationship we have with Christ.

How is your church? Is it full of love and does it follow after that love of Christ? Has it lost its first love? What are some ways to serve and share that love? Are you and your group so consumed with the work of Christ that Christ's sacrifice and provision is forgotten? Are you so busy serving that you forget to share? It can be very easy to get consumed with the work and service, but we must make it a priority to share about our faith as we live it.

The Poor Church, Revelation 2:8-11

Growing up on a farm I remember going to a small country church. I remember the narrow aisles, the uncomfortable pews, and the hymn books that stuck out of the backs of the pews that loved to slam into your knee caps as you found your seat.

However, I also remember some of the comments about the church members. The more popular one starting out with, "If we were only a bigger church and had the money."

How often do we hear or offer this excuse? Money can be a factor when starting a ministry, or in the general makeup of a church, but it should not be the determining factor. Money should not be the end all be all of a ministry. Many churches and ministries are very effective for the Kingdom of God, and they have little to no financial support.

The church in Smyrna was poor, small, and facing tribulation. Yet God said they were rich. I know many smaller churches that, because they are small or poor, feel like they cannot serve God or persevere through various tribulations.

These churches feel helpless, lost, outnumbered, understaffed, and overwhelmed with work. There is hope, God is our provider, and He has a ledger that is unlike any we have ever seen. Smyrna was poor by world's standards, but by God's standards was rich!

Not only was this church poor, they were being persecuted and going through tribulation. Could your church persevere through similar trials and tribulation? Would your faith be strengthened or would it be lost?

I know you are reading the passage and saying, "Hold up, Mark, this church was going to prison and dying. We don't have that in our church today." My response would be that you are correct. However, my question in return would be this: They were commanded to be faithful through their trials and tribulation in Smyrna, and yet we think that we do not have to be as concerned with being faithful today in America? Do we think we get a free pass? Do we take for granted the blessings that God has given us?

In America we are blessed to have the freedom of public worship. We are blessed to have nice buildings to gather together in while worshiping God. Yet there are tribulations that face the church that are, in some respects, even more dangerous than simply going to jail. There can be financial tribulation, complacency, attendance, pride, negativity, and a whole host of other issues that face the church today. Instead of overcoming them, we allow them to overtake us as a church, rendering that church ineffective and essentially dead.

A small budget allows God to prove his provision. A small church is better equipped to give personalized attention. It can be very easy to come up with a list of issues and problems. The real problem comes when the church and members lose sight of God's faithfulness and try to rely on their own resources. My hope and prayer is that small churches will not give in to the temptation of making excuses, and instead, focus on making disciples.

Matthew 28:19-20 says, "Go therefore and make disciples of all nations, baptizing them in the name of the Father and of the Son and of the Holy Spirit, teaching them to observe all that I have commanded you. And behold, I am with you always, to the end of the age."

Jesus did not say, "Hey guys, wait till you have a sweet sound system and some cool twirling lights before you start saying who I am or making disciples. "He said go and make some disciples. No excuses. So, right now, where you are at, in the town, neighborhood, and community, go make disciples and spread the word about Jesus.

I wonder what would happen if churches became satisfied with having a service on Sunday and Wednesday night and that was it? How would our society act? What would change? How would God's Word be shared? How would people come to know the Lord?

Look, the truth is that if this church in Revelation is considered to be poor and told to be faithful even in tribulation, then how much more should small churches, and all churches, be faithful and use what God has given? Any church that preaches and teaches God's Word is on the same side and all part of the body of Christ. Just because a forearm is bigger than a finger does not mean that the finger isn't important. We all have a job to do.

Ironically, this church along with the church in Philadelphia (Rev. 3:7) are the only two churches out of the seven that receive praise from God that was not followed by negative critique. God said good job and that was it. Even though they did not have everything going for them, they were faithful with what they did have.

Small churches can reach people and accomplish things that large churches cannot. Whether you belong to a big church or a small church, both are blessed with different types of missions and different tasks and opportunities. What kind of church do you belong to? Are you a person that comes up with excuses for not trying and serving? Or are you one who is faithful in what God has given?

The Wrong Church, Revelation 2:12-17

This is a touchy subject because it comes down to teaching and preaching and how some people argue about semantics and claim false teaching. For this section, I want to define what I mean by false teaching. False teaching is anything that is contrary to what is spelled out in the Bible. If it is in the Bible, then it is truth. And if someone is not preaching or teaching it as such, then they are wrong.

This church allowed false teaching to infiltrate their congregation. Reading in chapter 2 it shows how the church was strong and held to the name of Jesus Christ. Yet, as time went on, they allowed other lines of thinking and teaching to permeate the church. This epidemic runs rampant today in churches across America and the world.

For example, people wanting to be politically correct in the church would allow and give approval to a homosexual lifestyle. This is wrong and unbiblical. Just because it might be "legal" in all states does not make it legal and acceptable in God's eyes. Yet, as time goes on, people, *Christian* people, are becoming more and more accepting of this kind of lifestyle and choice (I say choice because there is no solid evidence to prove that people are born homosexual. It is a choice).[50]

That might be an extreme example, so how about a person who has grown up in the church their entire life and one day as a young adult they decide to live with a member of the opposite sex outside of marriage? There are churches out there that are okay with this kind of living. They even use sayings like, "Well, it's what all the people are doing these days." Or my favorite, "It makes sense financially."

I want to take a second and point out that even though God did not say, "thou shalt not live with the opposite sex before marriage," it is inferred that we as believers are to be

---

[50] There is not enough evidence for the genetic argument. I will not get into detail about this topic in this book. There are several theories about how it is genetic, but the scientific evidence is just not there.

set apart from the world, to guard our hearts, be sexually pure until marriage and to not do anything that could hinder our testimony.

So let me say this one more time for the record, if it goes against the Bible and God's Word, then it is wrong. If people are teaching that we should be accepting of this or anything contradictory to the Bible, then they are wrong as well.

I am not trying to come off as being hateful, proud, condescending, or on some soap box. I am also not saying that we as a church should teach or have hateful attitudes towards people who are not living a Biblical lifestyle. We should love them as people and show them God's love and how it is against His Word. We are to witness and bring them into God's family. With that said, part of being in God's family is to repent from those and other displeasing lifestyles and live a God-honoring life.

The problem I do have, and as shown in this and other passages throughout the Bible, is the issue of people teaching false doctrines and giving false information that can lead people away from God's truths. Sure, it is politically correct to be accepting of certain lifestyles, behaviors, and actions, but is God accepting?

We need to follow God and preach His truth and be a light in the dark world, exposing sin and lighting the way to the cross and salvation. This can go for a host of other issues, not just the big ones mentioned, but to the issue of pornography, gossip, hate, malice, slander, and a host of other issues that we often just try to ignore for the sake of peace and correctness.

I have seen and unfortunately been on both sides of some of these issues and have seen the devastation that can happen in the life of the person participating in the sin, but also the effect that it has on the church as they try to ignore the issues. We must draw and hold the line for the cause of Christ.

I pray that you are not one of these people preaching false doctrine and giving wrong information. I want to encourage you to stand up for what is right and stand up for the truth of Jesus Christ. Do not worry about what people think. You do not have to answer to them. God wants you to do what is right, even if it means correcting someone in a loving way when they are teaching the wrong thing. Maybe they just do not know the truth.

The Accepting Church, Revelation 2:18-29

This section ties in with the previous section. God, again, gives praise to the church about their love, faith, and works. The one thing God has an issue with is that they are accepting wrong teachings from a certain women.

Teaching was going on that, in layman's terms, was not what the Bible said at all. It included teaching that sex before marriage was okay, even sex after marriage with other people was okay, and to eat and drink whatever you wanted because it was all good and acceptable. It was the idea of, "Do whatever makes you feel good and makes you happy." Sounds familiar, right? Take a look at our society and listen to what people are saying.

Sexual immorality is running rampant in America, and if you think that it has not permeated the local church, then, my friend, you are sadly mistaken. There are more and more churches becoming accepting of, and even preaching the message of, "Do what makes you happy because God wants you to be happy."

Let's take a second and focus on just the adults in the church as an example. How many have been divorced and then remarried? How many have cheated on their spouse? How many adults reading this book have had more than one partner?[51] I am not trying to make anyone mad or feel guilty, because God has forgiven us all. However, I am trying to point out how our lives and experiences can impact the way we see the Bible and skew its teachings.

---

[51] Please do not fill in the blank or answer these questions out loud.

I remember talking to a gentleman who wanted to divorce his wife and he said that God wanted him to. He even went as far as trying to point out some biblical evidence trying to prove his point. In reality, he wanted to leave his wife for a new, younger woman, and he was trying to justify his actions.

As a side note on teaching right and wrong, adults with children, please be strong and be the parent of your child. I do not know how many parents I have seen getting their children contraceptives so that their children can go "have fun" without the consequences. God said wait until marriage, not "Go ahead, but don't get pregnant," or "Better have your daughter on the pill, just in case." You are the parent, not the friend. You are to raise your children in the right biblical truths (Prov. 22:6) not help them blend in with society.

I am a firm believer that most youth pastors do not get the help that they need. Think about it, how often does a young person go to youth group? They are with their friends in school day in and day out. They are with their sports team or music group, and then they are at church Wednesday night for an hour and church on Sunday for another hour. It is no wonder that our youth today are leaving the church to participate in all kinds of debauchery. Who has more influence? Who has more time with them?

A church is a group, a community of believers, and it is everyone's responsibility to help train and teach God's Word, not just the pastor. Please be active in your church. Make sure you know what is being taught inside the church and outside the church at school, in sports, in choir, and in your children's circle of influence.

Do not allow a false teaching to come into the church and fill people's minds with dangerous garbage. The best way to defend against it is to be active and make sure God's Word is being taught and learned by everyone, including you who are reading right now.

We must keep an attentive eye on what is being taught and what we are believing and not believing. We must filter everything through God's Word and see things through His eyes. It will not be easy, and it definitely can cause some hurt, but if we do not draw the line, then how do we know where the line is? How do we prevent our churches and its people from ending up like this church in Revelation?

How involved are you now with your church? Do you know who is teaching and what is being taught to your children and grandchildren? Are you willing to get up and get active for the Lord and defend the faith? What are some steps you are planning to take to make sure false teaching is not getting into the church? Are there people accepting certain behaviors and acts that you know should be stopped?

Not all churches are bad, but we should be aware and always keep an eye out because when we become content or start to get lazy, that is when things start to slip in. Take a moment and pray for your pastors and church leaders, that they would be diligent and faithful in what God has given to them. Pray for your church and those who are teaching in your church.

The Dead Church, Revelation 3:1-6

When I was first starting out in ministry, I was at a small country church near where I grew up. Within a few years of my arrival, the head pastor resigned from the church. I will not go into all the reasons why, but it had to do with his past some 30 years prior. At any rate, the elders held a private meeting. In that meeting they decided that they should get an interim pastor.

In the months that followed, the congregation attendance dropped from 150 on a Sunday to about 30. The interim pastor was not speaking from Scripture. In fact, when I approached him about it, he said he felt his job was to close that church because it was dying. It was at that point that I felt God saying get out, and I did.

It is always easier to let something die than it is to save it and try to bring new life back into it. This church in Revelation was dying. They did not have life in them at all, instead they were stagnant and not moving or growing towards Christ. They had been alive, they had been growing for Christ, but they got lazy, complacent, and careless, allowing everything to just die off.

It takes time, care, and patience to grow and to keep things alive. Growing up on a farm, you learn what it takes to grow plants and to take care of animals. When an animal gets sick, you have to take care of it. Taking care of it can be costly and expensive, but it is worth it in the end to see it get better and provide for the farm.

Same with a plant. It is easy to kill it, just don't water it. But if you take the time to water it, feed it and help it grow, then at harvest time, it will all pay off in the end.

The death of a church doesn't just happen in the small churches, it can happen in even the largest churches and organizations. The church and its members can be spiritually dying and not even know it. The pastor could be failing to feed the congregation, the congregation might not be active, and the list could go on all pointing to one thing, a dying church.

The hardest part about a stagnant church, one that is dying, is that there are always people saying things like, "Just let it die, its time has come and gone," or "All good things must come to an end." They would rather dig the grave and bury it than take the time to tend, nurture, care for, and see what God can do with the church.

If you are in a church that is stagnate and spiritually dying, then it is my prayer that you help breathe new life into it. Start praying, start serving, start asking God what He can do and what you should do so that His Kingdom can be expanded.

There is always time, God can use anyone and anything to accomplish his will. It is not too late, all has not been lost, God can breathe new life back into a church, and God can rescue the perishing and dying. God is God and nothing will be able to tear down what He has built up.

After I had left the church, the interim pastor decided to leave and a new pastor stepped into the pulpit. He made some changes and allowed God to use him however He needed, and now that church is starting to grow again. I want to encourage you that God has a plan for everything, just hold on and continue to serve to the best of your abilities. God will use you, God will revive, and God will breathe new life into His people again.

The Good Church, Revelation 3:7-13

This church got major praise from God. He even said, "I have loved you" in verse 9. This church has been faithful through everything. They held to God's promises and endured. This church didn't care about what other people thought. They were not worried about their reputation or their status. The things they cared about were keeping God's Word and not denying His name.

I know it is easy for us to rationalize that maybe they didn't have to deal with stuff like we do today, or maybe they were sheltered, maybe they were a mega church that was so big that they were invincible to the outside world. You could think that, but that would be wrong.

The church in Philadelphia was not a mega church, and although there was not a lot written about this church in the New Testament, we can know that they faced the similar problems that we do today because of how the other churches acted and what happened to them.

We also can tell a little about the society from reading Paul's writings and through other history books. This church faced similar problems that we face in our society today. We also know that they had little power.

This could mean that they just didn't have a lot monetarily or physically. In any case, they used what they did have for the work and glory of God.

Believers need to use what God has given them, not just pout about how they do not have the awesome lights, the 4KHD cameras, the thousand channel sound board and a whole team devoted to outreach. Society says that in order to minister, we need fill in the blank in order to have an effective ministry. Sadly, there are a lot of Christians that fall into this trap and then get depressed and stop trying because they do not have X, Y, and Z.

There is nothing wrong with having nice things, but at times this mentality can carry over to ministry. When that happens, we can become so overwhelmed with what we do not have that we lose sight of what we do have, which is the power, might, wisdom, grace, and knowledge of the Almighty God.

God didn't ask you to have everything under the sun to do ministry; what He is asking is that you use what you have now and serve Him with it. If you don't have a sound system, then talk louder. If you don't have a lighting system, then don't do stuff in the dark. Don't fall into the temptation that we have to compete with the secular world and obtain everything materialistic that we can to reach and preach the Gospel of Christ.

The Politically Correct Church, Revelation 3:14-22

In this passage of scripture, God really drops the hammer on this church. Although there is a lot of information and many sermons have been done on this passage, we will keep it to the main points. The main point that I would like to derive from this passage is that this church was, in essence, just a building.

This church was not on fire for God, it was not trying to reach and teach people, it was just complacent. This church is the perfect example of a politically correct church. This church didn't offend anyone, they didn't try to convert or teach the Gospel. They did however, meet and hang out and show off how much they had and how cool their possessions were. So let's make it relevant for today, let's try and picture a church that is like this in today's society.

Imagine a church with a beautiful design and layout. There is a large parking lot where everyone could get a great spot to park. Walking into the church, you see beautiful paintings and interior decorating that is comfortable and inviting. There is a full coffee bar where the coffee is free, ESPN is on the TV screen, and everyone is talking about their favorite movie or game they just saw.

Imagine that as you talk to people they say things like, "Oh, we have the greatest sound and light system in the whole state," or "We have the best music program, and the kids ministries are the greatest." You walk into the sanctuary and the temperature is perfect and the seats are comfy and can recline. The pastor gets up to the pulpit and gives a brief five to ten minute devotional in a soft soothing voice, and you are then dismissed to hang out with your friends.

Okay. Back to reality! Although some of those things would be nice to have, and that it is nice when people compliment a program or ministry, there has to be more than that. Church *cannot* be a superficial place. It cannot be an oversized coffee house or daycare facility. What would happen if no one ever grew in their relationship with God? What would happen if people were too concerned with what others thought than of what God thought?

Think of a church as a doctor's office. It is a place where we go for annual checkups and for physicals when we are sick. How would you like it if the doctor knew something bad was happening inside you and you could be harmed or even die, but he chose to tell you that everything was great? He didn't want you to feel bad, and he wanted you to like him, so he chose to tell you what you wanted to hear. I am not sure I would go back to that doctor, and I am sure you would not want a doctor like that.

So why is it that when it comes to our spiritual well being, we insist on wanting to only hear the good parts? Why do we, as churches and Christians, shy away from the truth and try to tell people what they want to hear? I know the pressure from society and other outside influences try to push us into only telling what they want us to tell them, but we need to stand up and preach the truth. Do not just be a lukewarm church trying to please everyone.

All too often I see or hear people telling stories of churches that are like the one we just imagined. The fact is that they do exist and are growing in number, that they are becoming more popular as people flock to them. Why wouldn't they? What is the harm? There are no hurt feelings there, no one stepping on your toes saying that you need to grow and mature in Christ.

How is your church? How are you? Are there areas in your life or your church that you sugarcoat? Do you or groups in your church try and only focus on what people want to hear? I know it is enticing to have people like you, to have people coming through the doors by the thousands, but the one question you must ask is this: Is telling people what they want to hear and gaining the popularity but neglecting God and the Bible worth it?

In America we have been blessed with the freedom to have church and to meet and pray where we wish. We have ample opportunities to serve and share our faith with those around us. What is holding us back? What are we doing as a church to ensure that we are following God's will, not our own?

As a church, are we taking advantage of the opportunities God has given us as a community of believers? Are we being careful and diligent to ensure that the correct teaching is being taught, that we are not losing our passion and becoming stagnant? How will we handle these and other situations that arise? How are we showing God's love and character through our church, to our communities, country, and world?

Discussion Questions

- What areas can you see that need improving in your church?
- Are you active in your church or just a person who likes to sit on the side line and complain?
- What steps can you take in making improvements?
- Are you willing to help and support your pastor as he leads and guides your church?
- Are you being a faithful steward in what God has given you to use in your church?

5

THE POLITICALLY CORRECT CHRISTIAN IN THE COMMUNITY

The community that surrounds the church should be the first mission field that the church witnesses and ministers to. With this in mind, why is it that there is such an emphasis placed on the mission field in some remote or undiscovered country? To live and witness in the exotic and untamed wild millions of miles away, yet forget our own back yard?

Please do not misunderstand me. I truly believe that we should preach, teach, and reach the lost in the farthest reaches of the world, and that we should support missions and the missionaries that are in every corner of the earth.[52] What I am trying to say is that Jesus was very specific in giving the great commission.

---

[52] I like the image of a stone being tossed in a calm lake. The ripple starts from the place of impact and goes out from there. How can we as Christians make a huge splash and ripples for Christ, if we cannot even create a ripple close to us?

Acts 1:8 says, "But you will receive power when the Holy Spirit has come upon you, and you will be my witnesses in Jerusalem and in all Judea and Samaria, and to the end of the earth."

Jerusalem was the city where the disciples were living. Judea was the country and Samaria was next door to Judea. We will be speaking more about this verse later on in the chapter, but I wanted to take a moment to point out how we are to proceed with our missions and how everyone can participate in missions.

The local community could be considered the easiest and most accessible mission field for every Christian. We already have established roles in the community with jobs, family, friends, children, and our very homes. God has placed each one of us in a circle of influence to best serve Him. So why then do we as Christians fall short and fail to witness, serve, and minister to our communities?

The temptation is to think of ministry as being out there far away, and we often miss the opportunities to serve in the here and now. I am reminded of the parable of the Good Samaritan, how some religious men of that time were so focused on other things or even themselves that they passed by and didn't help the needy. I think it would be of great benefit to take a moment and read that passage.

Luke 10:25-37 says, "And behold, a lawyer stood up to put Him to the test, saying, 'Teacher, what shall I do to inherit eternal life?' He said to him, 'What is written in the Law? How do you read it?' And he answered, 'You shall love the Lord your God with all your heart and with all your soul and with all your strength and with all your mind, and your neighbor as yourself.' And He said to him, 'You have answered correctly; do this, and you will live.' But he, desiring to justify himself, said to Jesus, 'And who is my neighbor?' Jesus replied, 'A man was going down from Jerusalem to Jericho, and he fell among robbers, who stripped him and beat him and departed, leaving him half dead. Now by chance a priest was going down that road, and when he saw him he passed by on the other side. So likewise a Levite, when he came to the place and saw him, passed by on the other side. But a Samaritan, as he journeyed, came to where he was, and when he saw him, he had compassion. He went to him and bound up his wounds, pouring on oil and wine. Then he set him on his own animal and brought him to an inn and took care of him. And the next day he took out two denarii and gave them to the innkeeper, saying, 'Take care of him, and whatever more you spend, I will repay you when I come back.' Which of these three, do you think, proved to be a neighbor to the man who fell among the robbers?' He said, 'The one who showed him mercy.' And Jesus said to him, 'You go, and do likewise.'"

I know this is kind of a long passage, but I would like to dissect it a little and show what a politically correct Christian would do and what a follower of Christ would do. First, I want to give you a little bit of background information on the people involved in this example Jesus was giving.

The Community

If you look at a map of where Jerusalem was in comparison to Jericho at the time of Jesus, you will notice a small winding road that links these two cities. This road was around 17 miles long and would descend close to 3,300 feet, mainly because Jericho is around 770 feet below sea level. Besides that, this road is a prime place for thieves to lay and wait for travelers to pass, so that they might relieve them of their possessions. One might say that in today's terms, it was a road that you would roll up the windows when driving through and make sure the doors were locked.

Just like in any community or city, there are busy places, clean places, safe places, and dangerous places. Since Jerusalem and Jericho were busy towns, business men would travel this road mentioned in the parable, making it a gold mine for thieves.

Another point that I would like to discuss at this time is that just like in any town or community, there was the issue of racism. It can be easy to think that issues like these never happened in biblical times, but they did, and they didn't try to hide it.

Think back to the 1950s and '60s when segregation was a huge issue in America, or think of a time when you witnessed racial tension and the outworking of it. Take that and multiply it by ten, and that would be the sentiment that was held between the Jews and Samaritans.

The Jews hated the Samaritans. In fact, they would try to avoid them at all cost. Keep this in your mind as you read the passage again.

The Man

There is not a lot of information given about the man who was robbed. He could have been a business man, a family man, or even a farmer. The only thing we know is that he was on the road traveling.

There is an assumption that I would like to make if you permit me. I would like to point out that in the story it didn't matter who the man was, what mattered was that the man fell into the hand of thieves.

He was minding his own business, doing his own thing, when suddenly tragedy struck him, and he was left on that road with nothing and left to die.

How many people do you know who are in your community that are walking down their road in life, doing their thing and minding their own business? What will happen to them when tragedy strikes? What will our reaction be?

The Priest

The priest was the first individual to pass by the wounded man lying on the side of the road. One would think that a priest would be filled with compassion and care for the suffering man on the road and would help him and pray for him. This was not the case.

There could be numerous reasons why the priest didn't want to help. It was still dangerous, there could have been more robbers and thieves waiting for him to stop and help the wounded man and then they would have robbed the priest as well. Another reason could have been that he did not want to defile himself by contact with the dead. He presumed that this man was dead, and so the priest refused to even come close.

Whatever the case may be, we can know that when the priest saw the injured man, he chose to walk on the other side of the road. He didn't even want to take time out of his schedule to help or even see if the man needed help.

How often are we like the priest? We don't want to get dirty, we don't want to take time out of our lives to even see if another person needs help. At times we get so busy and preoccupied with our own lives that we do not stop to tend to the needs of others on our path of life. Before we judge the priest, maybe we should all take a look in the mirror and see what is actually there.

The Levite

A Levite was a descendent of Levi from the Old Testament and out of the tribe of Levi. A Levite helped the priests with some of their duties and policing the temple. A Levite was not on the same level as a priest. Think of him as a head deacon or elder of a church, helping out where he could. Because the Levite was not on the same level as a priest, you could assume that he would have been more apt to help this man who had been left to die.

The issue of defiling himself with a dead person would have been less of an issue, although he could have been scared for his well-being. The main issue with these two characters was that even the most righteous and wise people can be enticed to neglecting and not loving our neighbors and community as God has commanded us to. We all are commanded to love and take care of those in need, to "get dirty" and help anyone and everyone who needs it and share the Gospel of Jesus Christ.

The Samaritan

The hero of our story, and the most unlikely hero is the Samaritan. Remember, Samaritans were hated by the Jews because of the history between them. In 722 B.C. the Jews were taken captive by Assyria. Assyria brought Gentiles (those who are not Jews) to live in the land they had just conquered, Israel. Some Jews stayed in the land and married the Gentiles and had children. I know you're thinking "What's the big deal," right? Well, the big deal is that according to Jewish law, only Jews could marry Jews, not gentiles.

Fast forward about 200 years and the Jews are returning to their home that they had been taken captive from and they find these half breeds, these descendants of the Jews and gentiles, and the pure Jews were mad. So the Jews called these impure people the Samaritans and hated them because they had intermarried and broken Jewish custom and law.

On the other side, the Samaritans didn't like how the Jews showed back up and tried to force their laws and customs on them. The feud between the two people started, and it only grew worse from there, to a point where there was no contact between the two people.

Now back to the parable. As Jesus was talking to this lawyer and group of people, Jewish people, He gives them two very likely people that would and should be prime examples of everything God wants. Instead, they come up short and now everyone listening is trying to figure out who could be coming next that could be a good example of loving our neighbor.

As they are sitting there, Jesus reveals the next traveling person to come upon our injured victim, and who could it be? TADA! It's a Samaritan. Remember what we just talked about, and how they hated each other? Well, they didn't forget, and they were stunned to hear that this Samaritan would be the hero in the story Jesus was giving.

What Jesus was trying to show and teach is that loving and caring is not always easy. It is not always clean or cheap, but it is worth it in God's eyes. Just like the Samaritan, we as Christians need to be active in our community and be willing to get dirty for Christ. It may cost us something, it may make us look odd or out of place, it may even force us to cross the racial barriers that we may struggle with.

None of these issues matter in God's eyes. We should not be politically correct in the community. Do not just walk to the other side of the road and expect someone else to come along and help. We are to step up and step out of our comfort zone to help and minister to those around us.

We should strive to witness, serve, minister, and help to make a positive change in our homes, communities, and local areas that we live in. We have been given great opportunities and freedoms to witness and share in our country. God has blessed us and we should take advantage of these freedoms and liberties to further His Kingdoms.

This leads me to another point that I would like to discuss about being politically correct in the community. There has been this weird and false theology that has been passed around that we, as Christians, are to just stay in our homes as hermits and not be active in our communities. That we are to submit to our government and not try to change it or vote against what the government wants. This should not be so.

God has placed each and every one of us in certain communities and areas of life to have and make an impact. Do not neglect or avoid it. Get out, get active, and get bold for Christ in your local neighborhood and community. Serve, help, vote, and try and make this place a better world and win people over for Christ.

I have a good friend who thinks that we as Christians should not vote or be active in the political process. I do not think that he is correct. In fact, we used to go round and around about this issue quite frequently. I never understood his point of view and it did not really make sense to me. However, there are some passages that lead toward how Christians should vote and be active.

> Romans 13:1-2 says, "Let every person be subject to the governing authorities. For there is no authority except from God, and those that exist have been instituted by God. Therefore whoever resists the authorities resists what God has appointed, and those who resist will incur judgment."

> Romans 13:5-7 says, "Therefore one must be in subjection, not only to avoid God's wrath but also for the sake of conscience. For because of this you also pay taxes, for the authorities are ministers of God, attending to this very thing. Pay to all what is owed to them: taxes to whom taxes are owed, revenue to whom revenue is owed, respect to whom respect is owed, honor to whom honor is owed." (Vote because God appoints those who rule)

> Deuteronomy 1:13 says, "Choose for your tribes wise, understanding, and experienced men, and I will appoint them as your heads." (We are to choose)

Proverbs 25:26 says, "Like a muddied spring or a polluted fountain is a righteous man who gives way before the wicked." (Don't give way to the wicked)

There are other passages that lend towards being active in that particular process. Basically it comes down to this: God has placed each one of us here and has given us certain freedoms to use for His glory. To misuse or even not use the gifts, abilities, and freedoms for God, is like a slap in the face saying, "Thanks, but no thanks, God."

A politically correct Christian thinks only of themselves and their convenience, blending in perfectly with the lost community around them, never stirring the waters, only trying to stay neutral.

I am not saying all Christians should constantly wave a Bible around in people's faces or have a huge cross in the yard so that all can see we are Christians. I *am* saying that by living our lives and being willing to take part in the community God has placed us in, those who are lost should see Christ and the cross in our lives.

Be willing to get your hands dirty, be willing to sacrifice and give, be willing to stand up and fight for what God would have you do.

Pray and have faith that God will provide and protect you as you serve and reach out into the community, neighborhood, and neighbors. It is commanded to love others as we would love ourselves. Show it, don't hide it.

What areas are there in your life right now that you know need improvement? Are you a Levite? The Priest? Or the Good Samaritan willing to give and do all for Christ? Are there people you know that are afraid of getting their hands dirty, afraid of upsetting the status quo and breaking the politically correct chains that our society has placed on us as Christians?

This is what I would like to call the "duh" section of this chapter. We as Christians need to witness to our neighbors and community. Duh, right? Well, it is easier said than done. I also struggle with this and have to make a conscious effort to witness to those around me and to those to who are in my circle of influence.

It is not only suggested, it is commanded that we witness to those around us as shown in Acts 1:8, which says, "But you will receive power when the Holy Spirit has come upon you, and you will be my witnesses in Jerusalem and in all Judea and Samaria, and to the end of the earth." This was one of the last things Jesus said before He ascended into heaven.

Notice how He threw in Samaria, telling it to His Jewish disciples? If you think that they didn't struggle with the concept, then you would be wrong. They were normal human beings like you and me. They just allowed the Holy Spirit to move in them and were willing to break the norms and social trends to serve Jesus and follow Him.

What I wanted to also point out at this juncture was that Jesus started with telling them to witness in Jerusalem, this, of course, being where they were. Yes, that's right, Jesus said, "Hey, start witnessing and talking about me right now in this area. And oh, by the way, see that town over there? Witness there too."

Jesus, the Son of God, did not just ramble off some towns that He knew. He purposely gave instruction to start witnessing about Him now and then move out from there.

As mentioned earlier, walk up to a pond as it is completely still, almost like a mirror as you look into the water, pick up a rock and toss it into the pond. You will see the splash and then the ripples that flow out from that stone that was tossed in the water.

Be that stone, take the plunge, and make the ripples! Allow God to use that ripple effect and impact so many more people than you may ever know. We just have to be willing to make the splash.

You're quite possibly thinking, "How am I supposed to witness? I didn't go to school for that. I will leave it to the preacher. I don't even know what witnessing means." I will give you a very simple definition that will help you out as it helped me out. Witnessing about Jesus is simply talking about Jesus. That's it, just talk about Him.

I have heard women talk for hours and never really know what they were saying, yet they can talk. Guys, before you start to laugh too hard, I have heard you talk for hours too. Don't believe me? Start talking about your golf game or the sports you watch or that new car you are saving for, maybe even a gun, fishing bait, or guitars.

My point is this: We all talk and communicate with numerous people on a daily basis. If we took an honest look at what we talk about, I am sure it rarely involves Jesus or even the church, unless it's making plans for after church.

We have all become masters of small talk and conversation that won't make anyone feel bad or awkward. In doing this, we fall short of the mark when doing what we are commanded, to talk about Jesus in our community.

I will caution you that when talking about Jesus, there can be consequences.

I remember when I was first out of college with my degree, my first job was in marketing. Every Monday the guys would come in and talk about how hung over they were and what all they did over the weekend or what they couldn't remember they did.

Often they would ask me how my weekend went, and I would proceed to tell them and then start sharing the message my pastor gave. After a few weeks I got called into the office of my boss, and he told me to be quiet and stop trying to share my faith or there would have to be some changes. I told him that every time the guys would share about their exploits, I would share about Jesus.

Changes were made. I changed from marketing at that company, to being a bag boy at a local grocery store. Now there were some other factors involved, but change did happen.

Looking back, I am glad they let me go. I didn't want to work at a place where I could not share my beliefs and what I had done that weekend. They were intolerant of me not being tolerant like them.[53] It was okay to show up to work late and be hung over, but heaven forbid that I talk about

---

[53] Personally I think it is almost an oxymoron when a person accuses another of being intolerant because they do not agree with that person. Are they not being intolerant of the other person and their disagreeing point of view? They accuse intolerance while being intolerant themselves!

how God was working in my life and what I had learned the day before at church.

I want to encourage you, God will provide. He says to witness to the lost. He will provide no matter what happens as long as we are faithful. It only takes a minute to talk about Jesus. I am not saying show up with a sign around your body screaming how everyone is going to hell and that the earth is ending, repent. Just talk, that's all, just talk about Jesus and what He has done and what He is doing.

Okay. Now that the duh part is over, I want to give some practical suggestions on how to witness in your local community and neighborhood, while not conforming to the political correctness that society says we should as Christians. These suggestions are also fun and everyone will enjoy them.

Throw a party

Get to know everyone. It doesn't hurt to make relationships with everyone. The food doesn't even have to be expensive, just hotdogs and chips with homemade lemonade and tea. Play Christian music in the background and have some fun games for the kids, maybe have a contest with a prize. Do something to have fun and get to know everyone; this will allow for time to talk and build relationships.

Have a book club/Bible study for the men or women in the community

Once you get to know everyone, maybe start having a regular gathering to discuss books or Christian books. You can invite everyone from an atheist to Muslim, from a Catholic to a Baptist. This, again, allows for conversation and building of relationships. It is also slightly better suited for conversation.

Celebrate the holidays

This is again fun and allows for time to know the neighbors. The easy ones are Christmas and Easter, but what about Halloween or the Fourth of July? A pastor of mine always has a party on Halloween. His Halloween party has become famous in his neighborhood. They will open the garage and have free chili and games for everyone, no costumes or decorations, they just have a fall theme and talk to everyone.

These are just a few examples of things you can do that are fairly cheap and allow you time to get to know the people God has placed around you, literally around you. Plus, parties are fun anyway. I mean who said being a Christian was boring? What other ideas can you think of that allow you opportunities to witness and just talk about Jesus and your faith and church? How could you change and make an impact on those around you or your church?

The politically correct Christian blends in like a chameleon to his surroundings and no one would ever know he was a Christian. Please do not blend in. Stand out, be a follower of Jesus Christ, be bold, and have fun. Maybe you will be able to come along and help out those who are scared to stand out and be politically incorrect for Jesus in the community.

Discussion Questions

- What are you doing to stand out?
- How are you living in your community that shouts and screams that Jesus is the Lord of your life?
- What kinds of activities could you do or become a part of to get active in your community and share Christ?
- Are you being a chameleon? Or are you standing out and standing up for your beliefs?

6

THE POLITICALLY CORRECT CHRISTIAN IN THE WORK PLACE

The work place can often be the easiest place to forget that we are Christians. Trying to fit in to get that desired raise and promotion, we are tempted to do almost anything so that we can achieve our goals. It is also at or near these moments that the devil really begins putting pressure on us to try and make us more susceptible to doing things in the work place we would not or should not do.

There is a temptation to get ahead in life or to get that promotion no matter what that often comes into play on the job. There is nothing wrong with trying to obtain a promotion or even to get ahead in life. The problem arises when we are willing to toss our coworkers, ethics, and even our morals under the bus in order to gain advancement and recognition in the work place.

I have had people come up to me and say, "Well, Mark, I have to swear or else the other guys will think I am weak. They won't take me seriously." Or, "I have to go out and drink with my coworkers and party with them because it makes the workplace more enjoyable." I even had a friend in marketing that told me that he "had" to go to strip clubs because that's where his clients wanted to go and do business.

Last time I checked, a loud club full of drunk and naked people is not exactly the best place to have a conversation and do serious business.

In this chapter, I would like to take some time and discuss some aspects and temptations that we as believers can and will encounter in the work place environment. There are several areas involving the work place that a politically correct Christian can thrive and show their true colors. I would like to take a moment and examine them.

A politically correct Christian can be lazy in the work place

Often the temptation is to give in and do the least amount of work possible at our place of employment just to get by Why not? With TV shows like *The Simpsons*, *Two and a Half Men*, *The Office*, or movies like *Office Space*, it's no wonder that society gives off the message to just be complacent, do the least, and you will be okay.

Colossians 3:23 says, "Whatever you do, work heartily, as for the Lord and not for men." This verse can be extremely encouraging, especially if you are not happy with your work conditions or your boss. I had a friend who pasted this verse on his cubical to constantly remind himself of who he was working for.

The flip side of this verse should be a challenge to work your hardest because you are working for the Lord. It can be hard to always do your best day in and day out. However, if we are working for God, anything less than our all is just pathetic.

If we are supposed to do everything as to the Lord, why are we only giving our partial best? A person who is concerned with being politically correct is more concerned with fitting in and doing the least instead of working hard for the glory of God.

I know what you are saying, "Mark, you don't know my job, it is meaningless and it stinks." I understand, believe me I have had similar and less than ideal work places as well. I would also have to say that God placed us in our jobs to have an impact. Regardless of whether it is a good job or bad one, we need to work for the Lord, and we cannot do that when we are lazy and just trying to "slide" through life.

A politically correct Christian will speak the same language in the work place

When I am talking about work-place language, I am not referencing the technical lingo and terminology needed and used in that work environment. Please do not start using your own terminology if you work in a hospital or at a car shop or anything like that, it would be bad for the rest of us. Can you imagine if a surgeon just started making up their own language during a surgery? "Nurse, hand me the doodly-booper and the shiny loopty-loop." That would be disastrous.

If your work place uses specific terminology, please keep using that. I am not saying that we should forget all our education and not use correct terminology in the work place. I am also not saying that we should revert back to the New King James English at our work place either. How weird would that be? "Oh, Tim, wouldst thou bringeth me thy stapler so that I might useth it and then returneth it in a fortnight?"

What I am saying is that we as Christians need to be careful about the colorful language that is often used in the work place. You know what I am talking about, the vulgar jokes, or that one joke where the person looks around before he starts telling it.

If you participate in the joke or even just listen and laugh, it is just the same as if you said it yourself and you can lose your ability to witness. I am saying this to myself as much as anyone. Those who know me know I love humor and jokes as much as anybody, and I have been guilty of laughing at some questionable jokes before.

I am not saying do not have a sense of humor. I think God loves a sense of humor. However, I do want to urge caution. If you cannot say the joke or laugh at the joke in church, then don't say it or laugh about it at all.[54]

Humor can ease tension, lighten a mood, make one feel better and even unite and bring friendship together. However it can also alienate, strengthen stereotypes and racial prejudices, as well as objectify and destroy a person or their beliefs. One must be careful with humor. One wrong joke and a testimony could be ruined forever in that work place. Here are some verses that will help bring home my point.

> Ephesians 5:4 says, "Let there be no filthiness nor foolish talk nor crude joking, which are out of place, but instead let there be thanksgiving."

> Colossians 4:6 says, "Let your speech always be gracious, seasoned with salt, so that you may know how you ought to answer each person."

---

[54] I have to give my wife credit for that statement.

Proverbs 26:18-19 says, "Like a madman who throws firebrands, arrows, and death is the man who deceives his neighbor and says, 'I am only joking!'"

The other language that I would like to talk about is the more obvious one, that of foul, vile words. You know, the ones that your mom would wash your mouth out with soap for saying? It is my opinion that there are quite a few Christians that even today need to have their mouths washed out with soap.

Just because one is a Christian does not mean that they are immune to this type of language. It happens so subtly that unless you are carefully looking for it, one day you will be swearing with such fluidity and ease that you will not even know how it happened.

I know you could blame it on your surroundings or say it just happened, but what if Jesus used that excuse? What if at the garden right before Jesus is taken to the cross He is praying to God and saying, "Sorry, God, I know I was supposed to be perfect and all, but you know my surroundings and everything. I just sinned you know, it just happened." Well, it didn't happen that way, and thank God it didn't! Jesus was sinless and perfect, and He did not allow His surroundings to impact or change Him.

A politically correct Christian allows himself to be changed and influenced by his coworkers and environment, instead of changing and impacting those for Christ. The politically correct Christian is *weak*. We are commanded to witness (see chapter 5) and to impact the world that we live in. If your excuse is that you were just overwhelmed, then take a second and read this.

> 1 Corinthians 10:13 says, "No temptation has overtaken you that is not common to man. God is faithful, and he will not let you be tempted beyond your ability, but with the temptation he will also provide the way of escape, that you may be able to endure it."

> Hebrews 2:18 says, "For because He Himself has suffered when tempted, He is able to help those who are being tempted."

> James 1:2-3 says, "Count it all joy, my brothers, when you meet trials of various kinds, for you know that the testing of your faith produces steadfastness."

There is no excuse. When we come face to face with God we will try and make excuses, and there will be none. Believe me, I can be the king of excuses, but God and His Word refutes any reason why we would sin.

Every temptation we come across, we are provided a way out and given strength (that doesn't mean it will be easy) to overcome and escape that situation, if we want to.

Another area regarding language that often is overlooked and yet is more prevalent than other forms of language would be that of gossip. Gossip is not as easily identifiable as, say, cursing or sharing a vulgar joke.

Gossip can be devastating and elusive as we strive to tame the tongue. We have become masters at gossip. We can justify it, mask it, and can cover it up in shrouds of concern, prayer requests, or even care for the individual and situation.

A politically correct Christian can use gossip like a skilled painter uses a paint brush. The elegant strokes and shading on the canvas will depict such a masterpiece that people forget the mess that it might have left in the process of making that painting.

Gossip can be like that painting, appearing like it is beautiful and a true work of art. However, unlike art, that can be a thing of lasting beauty, the mess and disaster of gossip cannot be so easily cleaned up by paint thinner and water.

Psalms and Proverbs are full of verses that speak to the issue of gossip.

Psalm 34:13 says, "Keep your tongue from evil And your lips from speaking deceit."

Psalm 141:3 says, "Set a guard, O LORD, over my mouth; Keep watch over the door of my lips."

Proverbs 11:13 says, "He who goes about as a talebearer reveals secrets, But he who is trustworthy conceals a matter."

Proverbs 20:19 says, "He who goes about as a slanderer reveals secrets, Therefore do not associate with a gossip."

We must be careful and on guard to not only identify gossip, but also put an end to it as it permeates our workplace, homes, lives, and even our churches. A politically correct Christin will use gossip to get ahead in the workplace and have personal gain through the use and implementation of gossip.

One other thing I would like to quickly mention in regards to language is that especially at work, a politically correct Christian will be quick to complain and grumble about work and surroundings. But if you will permit me to give a verse, you will see how foolish it is, and that a faithful Christian should be quiet and follow God.

Proverbs 29:11 says, "A fool gives full vent to his spirit, but a wise man quietly holds it back."

Just because it is easy to complain does not mean we should. Please do not misunderstand me. If you are put in an unsafe or ethically compromising situation or you feel that the company is doing something it shouldn't, then it is okay to talk to someone in charge. This is different from just complaining every day about the coffee, the short break, the uncomfortable chairs, or having to get up early every day.

I know that the temptation is there, it even seems harmless and can be easily justified, but we must be on guard. The work place can be the most impactful place of planting seeds and sharing our testimony and witness. We must be careful, we must be strong, we must not give in to foul language and other forms of unchristian behavior.

A politically correct Christian will fight the same fight in the workplace

What do I mean by fight the same fight? I mean that it is extremely tempting to fight fire with fire. When a coworker bashes on you or tries to make you look bad, our gut instinct is to push back even more.

I am reminded of a movie quote that really sums this thought up. This quote is from the movie *The Untouchables* where the character Malone, played by Sean Connery is explaining how to get the bad guy, Al Capone. Malone says,

You want know how to get Capone? They pull a knife, you pull a gun. He sends one of yours to the hospital, you send one of his to the morgue. That's the Chicago way! And that's how you get Capone.

I like the movie, I just do not think that mentality is the godliest way to handle a situation.

This is often the mentality we have when it comes to office politics and confrontation in the work place. I am reminded of the example of Jesus when he stood before his accusers in Matthew 27:11-14 and as they accused him, he kept silent and did not talk back to them or even zap them with some lightning bolts to show his power. He stood there and took it, as it was stated in Isaiah 53:7.

I know that Jesus was sent here to die for us and so He was fulfilling that promise, but He was also fully human and had human reactions. We as Christians are to follow the example of Jesus and strive to live like He did, not just on Sunday, but every day, even in the work place.

There is something I would like to bring to your attention that is a little troubling to some and a number of people have disagreed with me on, and actually gotten very upset with me about. I am a firm believer that if you are not willing to give up your job for Jesus Christ, then you are placing that job ahead of Him and making it your priority over God.

Let me explain. I understand that there are times when careers require traveling over a weekend, thus missing a church service here or there. However, when your job takes over and you are missing more and more worship services and opportunities to serve at your local church, then maybe it is time for a change.

Far too often careers can take priority over our lives, family and marriage included. Often unfaithfulness happens when away from home. I have found that many divorces occur as a result of people placing their careers and all that it entails ahead of their spouses.

I cannot count the number of marriages destroyed by a workaholic, the number of children that cry because mommy or daddy are not there for them due to the work they are choosing to be a part of. How many church events are understaffed because people said they would help and serve until work got in the way? How many meals left uneaten, pictures untaken, and memories never made? When work becomes your number one priority in life, then it is time for a new job.

Looking at Matthew chapter 5 and corresponding parts in the Gospels. There is a very important trend that I would like to point out. Jesus called his disciples. What is interesting is that there were a variety of different men called, from fishermen to tax collectors and everything in between.

What I specifically want you to notice is this: When Jesus called, they immediately left and followed Him. No matter what profession a believer is in, when the call of Jesus is heard, we should follow and not delay.

The question is: What is God calling you to do? In the very simplest of answers, God is calling you to do what you are doing now, but for His glory and in His way.[55] If you are a parent, then God called you to be the best godly parent you can be. What are you doing right now that God is calling you to do? What is hindering you from fulfilling that call?

I can hear you saying, "Mark, you don't know how many bills I have," or "I will just do this for a little bit to get ahead, it's what I have to do." My response is this: When we have a mentality of "This is what I have to do to provide and have a good life," then we are taking our reliance and trust from God and placing it on ourselves. Maybe we are just too busy trying to have a good life that we forget what real life is. We should take initiative and strive to work our hardest to provide, but never forget who the real provider is: God.

Proverbs 3:5 says, "Trust in the Lord with all your heart and lean not on your own understanding." If we truly believe that the Bible is God's Word and we believe in God, then why is it so hard to apply this to our careers? Why does

---

[55] Isaiah 55:8

Christianity, the Bible, and our belief in God's Word stop at the entryway of our jobs and careers?

If you cannot trust God to provide for you fully, then how can you say that you trust God at all? If you are afraid of losing your job or missing out on the promotion because of your faith and beliefs, then how can you sing the song, "I Surrender All"? The song "I Surrender All" becomes "I Surrender Some, as Long as it Does Not Affect My Work, My Comfort or My Life."

There is an old hymn and many current worship songs that both have this in common and go along these lines saying, "I would rather have Jesus than anything this world affords today."[56] We sing songs like this in church, and yet once we step outside the church, we start to worry and allow ourselves to get into the rat race of life, willing to do anything to get ahead.

Another argument that I often hear in regards to the work place getting "in the way" of ministry is this one: "God doesn't call everyone into full-time ministry. God's not calling me, so I don't have to go, I can just work my job and live my life." I, again, would have to disagree. God calls everyone into full-time ministry. He might not call everyone into being a

---

[56] Rhea Miller, George Shea, "I'd Rather Have Jesus" in *The Celebration Hymnal, Songs and Hymns for Worship*, Eds. Tom Fettke, Ken Barker, Camp Kirkland (USA: Word/Integrity, 1997): 506.

pastor or minister or teacher or missionary, but He has called everyone to be missionaries right where they are at in life. The greatest missionary, Paul, also worked a secular job in construction as a tent maker.

I want to take a moment and ask the question, what would you be willing to do to get a promotion at your work place? I want you to pause and really think about this. Be honest, if your boss or even the owner of the company came to you and said they would promise you whatever you want from the company if you only compromised yourself a *little*, would you do it?

Or how about if your boss came to you and said if you didn't perform a questionable/illegal act, you would be fired with no benefits or severance package, would you do whatever it is that they are asking? Would you be willing to give up that job? Or would you compromise your faith, ethics, and morals just to get ahead or to survive?

God can and does use people in all walks of life. A politically correct Christian tries to leave God out of his work. Welcome God into your work place, allow Him and the message of His son to flow in everyday work conversation. You have opportunities in your work place that no one else has: take full advantage of that.

I remember as a young boy I was playing in our house in the afternoon and my dad came home. I know it was in the early afternoon because cartoons were not on yet, and my mom told us to go outside and play. Walking outside, I passed my dad and saw that he had a big box with him that was filled with miscellaneous stuff and some pictures of us that he had from his office.

Later that night as we were sitting at the dinner table, it was explained to us that dad had lost his job, but that we were going to be okay. It wasn't until later in life that I found out why my dad had lost his job at that company. My dad was a computer programmer and he was working his way up in the company.

He was honest, hardworking, and really good at what he did for that company during his time there. There were no problems until his coworkers and some superiors wanted to go golfing during business hours and on the company's dime. Kick back and enjoy some cold drinks and have fun as someone else picked up the tab, what more could you want? Well, my dad said that he didn't want to be included in that because he thought it was wrong. As a result for standing up for his beliefs and ethics, they eventually became annoyed and eventually fired him.

There were some tough times at the Taylor home when my dad was unemployed, but I was and still am proud of my dad for the stand he took and for how he continues to strive to follow God and be a godly husband and father. I am not saying my dad is perfect, but I am saying that he was willing and is still willing to lose any employment he has in order to follow God and His Word.

Are we as believers and Christians willing to follow God in the workplace? Are we willing to trust God or trust our savings account? Are we willing to follow God as our leader or only follow our flawed *human* bosses and leaders?

I would like to take a second and address those who are in leadership. Whether you are in a leadership position now or will be in the future, I would like to share with you a verse that really resonated with me in regards to leadership. This verse is found in Colossians 4:1 where it says, "Masters, treat your bondservants justly and fairly, knowing that you also have a Master in heaven."

There are other numerous verses about being a leader. I would like to share a few more of them so that I may get a few points across about how a Christian should be a leader.

Proverbs 31:8-9 says, "Speak up for those who cannot speak for themselves, for the rights of all who are destitute. Speak up and judge fairly; defend the rights of the poor and needy."[57]

Matthew 20:26 says, "Not so with you. Instead, whoever wants to become great among you must be your servant."[58]

Luke 12:48 says, "Everyone to whom much was given, of him much will be required, and from him to whom they entrusted much, they will demand the more"

Titus 1:7-9 says, "Since an overseer manages God's household, he must be blameless—not overbearing, not quick-tempered, not given to drunkenness, not violent, not pursuing dishonest gain. Rather, he must be hospitable, one who loves what is good, who is self-controlled, upright, holy and disciplined. He must hold firmly to the trustworthy message as it has been taught, so that he can encourage others by sound doctrine and refute those who oppose it."[59]

For those who are in leadership positions, Luke 12:48 should be a very sobering reminder that your position, whatever it is, should not be taken lightly. I must confess that

---

[57] *New International Version*. Colorado Springs, CO: International Bible Society, 1984. Print.
[58] Ibid.
[59] *New International Version*. Colorado Springs, CO: International Bible Society, 1984. Print.

I have been guilty of taking my responsibilities lightly at times, but this verse reminds me of how leaders will be required to give.

Working in retail since the age of 14 and through college, I met a lot of different people and worked under a lot of different supervisors. It is astounding how people can take the same position or title and do weird things with it and go the extreme. I had one boss that would never clean or work, he made everyone else do it, and he would just bark orders and sit in the back room. I had another boss that was always working and trying to do everything himself and not delegating anything to anyone.

Being a leader is difficult. It is not about barking orders or trying to get everything done yourself, and it isn't about being a slave driver and cracking the whip. Being a leader is about being humble and having a servant's heart trying to work with those around you to accomplish the job at hand for Christ's glory, not our own.

It also means sticking up for those who work under your supervision, being fair and honest with them and making sure that they are taken care of. As a leader in a supervisory role, your needs should come last. Take responsibility and protect those who work for you and with you, be a servant leader. Be strict, but compassionate, just, but forgiving. Use your position to show God's love to those around you.

A Christian leader or a leader who is a Christian, should know this and strive to be fair and just, following God's Word in the work place. There is a lot of information about being a leader. There are also leadership programs and materials that local churches can participate in and be a part of, (you can ask your pastor about the resources available.)

Speaking of pastors, they are leaders themselves. There is a joke around most churches that the pastor has it easy because he only works on Sundays.[60] Pastors are leaders of their church, placed there by God. Your pastor, regardless of his faults or downfalls, has one of the most challenging and demanding jobs on earth. We need to be praying for our pastors every chance we get, even if you don't like his jokes on Sunday mornings.

For those who are about to become supervisors or leaders, take a moment to reread Titus 1:7-9. Just because these examples are in the Bible does not mean that they were only for biblical times. Strive to accomplish these biblical qualities and strive for what is good. It will be noticed. Sometimes it will cause problems because doing what is right can make people upset, but would you really want to work at a place where doing what is morally and biblically right is frowned upon?

---

[60] Most pastors actually work six to seven days a week and are on call 24/7.

I also want to encourage those who are on the way up the success ladder to please be careful. It can be easy to lose sight of what is right and what is wrong and most importantly what *God* says. Also, if you are a strong Christian and God is blessing you with promotions and you are having an impact on those around you, I encourage you to enjoy, but keep a lookout. Satan attacks those who are serving God and making a difference.

We can understand this by looking at the life of Adam in Genesis as God called him to have dominion over the earth. As Adam and Eve had their relationship with God and were doing as God had commanded, Satan came onto the scene and has been doing the same thing ever since.[61]

Satan's attacks are never obvious either. It may start out as having a harmless lunch with a secretary or assistant, it may even be with good intentions such as driving someone home after work if their car is broken down. Satan works within the subtleness of life. One thing leads to another, and next thing you know, your life is in shambles, you have forgotten God, and you are standing there trying to figure out what happened. I pray this never happens to you.

---

[61] You can also look at the life of Job and Paul, or look at 1 Peter 5:8-9

Finally, for those who are not a supervisor or in a position of authority, those who work day in and day out for another person, I want to encourage you by saying that God has a reason for placing you where you are. Remember when He delivered the Israelites out of Egypt? How hard did they have it at work? I want to challenge you to be an ambassador for Christ, share His love, and pray for your supervisors. Just because you are not in charge doesn't mean you can't make a difference in people's lives.

I want to encourage you with this verse again from Colossians 3:23 which says, "Whatever you do, work heartily, as for the Lord and not for men." This verse can make a huge difference in your life. When work is hard and the supervisor is being a jerk, just remember you are doing it for God, not him or her. When things are not going your way and people at work are just plain annoying, remember you are working for God, not them.

God has appointed every person to a certain position and place in life to serve Him. Some He gave to lead, others to follow, but remember we all follow the one true God, and as believers, we are all brothers and sisters in Christ. Pray for those in charge, help those under your supervision, work for the Lord, not to man, and serve God with all your heart.

A politically correct Christian will always take the easy way out. They will blend in and do whatever it takes to get ahead in life, even if it means sacrificing their testimony and beliefs. They may seem to be happy in the here and now, but it's not this life that matters, it's the next, and that is where the faithful will receive their reward. Pray for those Christians who have lost their way and are more caught up with society and being politically correct than following God. We are all God's family and we should be ready and able to pray for those who God has placed in our lives.

What steps can be taken to ensure that Satan will not get a foothold in our lives, specifically in the work place? Are we being careful of our actions, words, and attitudes in the work place? How can growth and accountability occur in your work environment? Is there at least one person that you know that you could witness to this week? In what specific area, relating to your job, can you be praying for? Or have others pray for?

Discussion Questions

- Are you the same person in the work place as in church?
- Are you striving to live out your personal beliefs and Christian values/principles at work?
- What steps can you take to help you be a bolder Christian in your work place?
- What areas or things about your work can you specifically pray for?
- Is your work getting in the way of church, family, or God?

7

THE POLITICALLY CORRECT CHRISTIAN AND MONEY

This subject can be a sensitive one, a hot topic for some, and a do or die for others. There have been numerous books, seminars, classes, and sermons on this subject. For a little while, these learning tools impact people and the way that they think about money, but often only temporarily.

In this chapter, I would like to look at what the Bible says about money and what we as Christians actually do with money. My disclaimer before we get too far into this is that this chapter is not all-encompassing. It is more of an overview of the financial situation in a Christian's life and how Christians handle the provisions and money that they maintain.

I would like to address for a moment those who think that God is not interested in how we conduct our business or how we handle the finances and provisions that God gives us. I am reminded of two parables that are given in Matthew and Luke.

The first is in Matthew 25:14-30, but the second parable in Luke 19:11-27 is the one I would like to take a look at more in depth and would like you to read. Luke says,

> As they heard these things, He proceeded to tell a parable, because He was near to Jerusalem, and because they supposed that the Kingdom of God was to appear immediately. He said therefore, "A nobleman went into a far country to receive for himself a Kingdom and then return. Calling ten of his servants, he gave them ten minas, and said to them, 'Engage in business until I come.' But his citizens hated him and sent a delegation after him, saying, 'We do not want this man to reign over us.' When he returned, having received the Kingdom, he ordered these servants to whom he had given the money to be called to him, that he might know what they had gained by doing business. The first came before him, saying, 'Lord, your mina has made ten minas more.' And he said to him, 'Well done, good servant! Because you have been faithful in a very little, you shall have authority over ten cities.' And the second came, saying, 'Lord, your mina has made five minas.' And he said to him, 'And you are to be over five cities.' Then another came, saying, 'Lord, here is your mina, which I kept laid away in a handkerchief; for I was afraid of you, because you are a severe man. You take what you did not deposit, and reap what you did not sow.' He said to him, 'I will condemn you with your own words, you wicked servant! You knew that I was a severe man, taking what I did not deposit and reaping what I did not sow? Why then did you not put my money in the bank, and at my coming I might have collected it with interest?'

And he said to those who stood by, 'Take the mina from him, and give it to the one who has the ten minas.' And they said to him, 'Lord, he has ten minas!' 'I tell you that to everyone who has, more will be given, but from the one who has not, even what he has will be taken away. But as for these enemies of mine, who did not want me to reign over them, bring them here and slaughter them before me.'"

This parable in Luke comes right after Jesus meets Zacchaeus the tax collector. As they are sitting there in Zacchaeus's house, Jesus starts telling a story about money, this being something that a tax collector would understand. So Jesus gives the story about the ten minas and how we should be diligent until the Lord comes back.

This story in Luke is different from the one in Matthew in that ten minas was a much smaller amount than talents. A mina was probably worth about a sixtieth of a talent, so this was not a lot of money in comparison. Yet the point was still given and made about how we as servants should handle the responsibility of what God has given to us as believers.

There is no sin in having a lot of money if you use it wisely for the Lord and for His will. Look in verses 16-17, because the servant was faithful in a little, the master gave him more.

I have often wondered why or how some Christians believe that having wealth is wrong and sinful. I have never found a passage to support that line of thinking, yet it prevails in our Christian circles.

There is something to be said about having stuff just to have it, or amounting up wealth to show off and waste it on frivolous things. Again, not to say that you cannot have nice things; however, I believe that if God chooses to bless a person and that they are faithful with what God has given them, then we as fellow believers should not condemn them for their success.

On the flip side, look at the end of the story. The last servant didn't do anything with what the master had entrusted to him. He wasted his time holding it to himself and not using it to gain anything else. Did you notice the response the master had for him? It wasn't very good.

Before I get to the next topic, I would like to mention that this parable is about what God gives us as His children. Talents, skills, knowledge, status, financial blessings, and so on are all given by God to us to use for Him. If we fail to use what He has given to us, no matter how little or how great, we will be wasting the blessing that He has given to us, like the last man in the parable of Luke.

It has always been frustrating for me to see talents or gifts being wasted and resources sitting unused. I cannot tell you how many churches God has blessed with land, a large building, a great location, or a smart tech team. The church, more often than not, sits on it all, allowing weeds to grow up, dust to collect, and the talented volunteers to get discouraged and give up.

It is sad when this type of action happens. It is sad when God has given so much skill and talent to believers, and they waste it instead of giving it to the Lord and allowing Him to use them for His glory and honor. Whether you are a skilled craftsman or an artist, musician, writer, cook, or teacher, please do not waste your talents; give them to the Lord and do it for His glory.

I am not saying that we will all be recording artists or talented painters or world renowned mega church pastors, but that is not why we do what we do. We should do everything for the glory of God regardless of the payoff or lack thereof. I wonder how sad or upset God gets when we as believers waste our abilities and gifts?

Not only should we offer ourselves to God and his service, but we are to also give financially to the work and ministry of God. This strikes a chord with some people, you know who you are, the ones who say "I will volunteer my time, but giving up my money? Not happening."

Sadly this can be an accurate example of how people think. In the book, *Crazy Love*, Francis Chan talks about how Christians or lukewarm Christians like to just give "leftovers" to God.

You know how it goes. The offering plate comes by and you frantically search your pocket or purse for something to throw in the plate. You push aside the pen and paper, get rid of the pocket lint, take out everything in your purse (I think only God knows what exactly is in a woman's purse) and you find some change. Like Rocky after a fight, you toss the change in the plate and feel like a champion.

Is that really what it is and what it means to give an offering? God is not a beggar out on the street with a cup asking for change. He isn't asking for quarters to do His laundry. Our God, the creator and sustainer of all life being perfect and holy, offering His only Son as a payment for our sin is asking for our tithes and offerings. He is asking for your best.

I want to take a moment and define two terms I just used so that we may all be on the same page as we continue our conversation.

Tithe: Originally meaning a tenth, or ten percent. In Deuteronomy, part of worship was that of giving, and a tithe was taken out annually. According to Numbers, the people of Israel gave a tithe to the Levites in return for their priestly service.

Offering: In the simplest of terms, an offering is anything above and beyond what a tithe would be.

Before you get carried away with your calculator trying to figure out what ten percent is in your budget, I would like you to read a passage of scripture in regards to offerings.

Mark 12:41-44 says, "And He sat down opposite the treasury and watched the people putting money into the offering box. Many rich people put in large sums. And a poor widow came and put in two small copper coins, which make a penny. And He called His disciples to Him and said to them, 'Truly, I say to you, this poor widow has put in more than all those who are contributing to the offering box. For they all contributed out of their abundance, but she out of her poverty has put in everything she had, all she had to live on.'"

This passage always gets to me and there are a few things worth pointing out.

First is that people could see what was being offered; there was no unmarked envelop to drop into the offering plate. Everyone could see what was given. Second is that even though she was poor, she gave.

By now you're thinking "Duh, she gave, Mark, that's what the Bible said." My point is that it must have hurt her to give that much. What she was giving was what she needed for food and provisions for the day and possibly the next day. She gave and she had faith that God would provide.

I would like to put this story into today's time frame. There are two people, both are Christians, one is rich and the other is poor, like, he has to save up to buy off the dollar menu poor.

Sunday comes around and it is time for the offering, they ask the rich man to stand and give the prayer and he does and adds how God has blessed him. He is going to give $1,000 for today's offering. The poor man sitting in the back is quiet, but when the plate comes around he puts in his only dollar, it is crumpled up and dirty, but it is the only paper bill he has.

God is pleased when we give, not just a little, but when we give until it hurts. I am not saying it is bad to have money and be well off, thank God that He has chosen to bless you in that way. However, because God has blessed you in your finances, allow God to search your heart and ask Him if you are giving your all to Him, giving until it hurts. The rich man gave a $1,000. So what? He had millions in his bank.

There is a huge difference between those who give because they have to and those who give because they want to. Those who give sacrificially and those who give sparingly. Those who are capable of giving out of poverty, trusting God to provide or those who rely on themselves and believe they are somehow helping God out with their offerings.

God is not asking us to all be poor and beg for everything. On the contrary, we are to be responsible to bless others as God has blessed us. The point that I am trying to get across is this: God gives and provides everything to us. Part of worship is to give back to Him, give sacrificially, and trust that He will continue to provide for our needs.

We in America have plenty, we are blessed beyond belief in comparison to much of the rest of the world, and yet we still are very cautious of giving money. There are people who own multiple homes and own boats to use once a year, but will only give five dollars to the work of God. There are people who own fleets of cars and more items than they can count, yet only give a little here and there.

Instead of having more junk sitting around your home, instead of buying stuff to fill our lives and our time, instead of placing so much value in our "tangible" items, give it to God. That is what sacrificial giving is. Instead of getting what you want all the time, consciously give that to God and allow Him to use that for the furtherance of His plan and His Kingdom.

That is the difference between a worldly Christian who is more concerned with appearances and having the latest and greatest, and a Christian that has their mind set on their treasures in heaven. It seems that a politically correct Christian will give a little and then break their arm trying to pat themselves on the back as they let people know just how much they gave.

Sometimes, it is not so much about the money as it is dealing with and managing the money. How you manage your money is a great indicator of how you manage your beliefs, faith, and what you place your trust in. For example, if you said that you trusted the stock market, yet never placed a penny in there, did you really trust the market?

I remember when I was first starting out in my adult life, I would always struggle to find money to give in the offering. Internally I knew I was to give, and I would wrestle with myself every week, but physically the money just was not there. I made a good living, even through college, I just didn't know how to manage my money as best as I could. I failed to make God my priority over my money.

Sadly, some Christians, and that number is growing, do not know how to properly handle money and do not make God their priority in their financial lives. They spend it frivolously and cannot manage their own budget. I am not merely talking to high school and college-age people, but to the adults who cannot handle a credit card or stick to a budget.

If I had a nickel for every adult I saw that needed help with their finances, I would never have to work a day in my life. The amount of self-help books is astounding, and books on budgeting and financial planning books are becoming ever more popular. There are a few good resources that can be very helpful, just be cautious because there is a lot of junk out there.

I am not saying that I have it mastered (my wife knows I love to spend money), but I am blessed to have a family that is very keen on finances. There are some basic biblical truths about running your finances that are worth taking a look at and understanding.

First, always give to God because He provides and gives us everything we have, even our very breaths. In Mark 12:13-17, Jesus answers some questions thrown at him regarding finances.

Mark 12:13-17 says, "And they sent to Him some of the Pharisees and some of the Herodians, to trap Him in His talk. And they came and said to Him, 'Teacher, we know that you are true and do not care about anyone's opinion. For you are not swayed by appearances, but truly teach the way of God. Is it lawful to pay taxes to Caesar, or not? Should we pay them, or should we not?' But, knowing their hypocrisy, He said to them, 'Why put me to the test? Bring me a denarius and let me look at it.' And they brought one. And He said to them, 'Whose likeness and inscription is this?' They said to him, 'Caesar's.' Jesus said to them, 'Render to Caesar the things that are Caesar's, and to God the things that are God's.' And they marveled at Him."

One thing I want to bring to your attention about this passage is this: we are to give back to God what is God's. The logical question that should have been asked or that people should ask now is what is God's. The answer is simple. In Genesis 1:27 we read that we were created in the image of God. God chose to make us in His image, having His imprint on us, and to set us apart from all other creation. Just like a person can look at a dollar bill and see a person's image, so people should look at Christians and see God's image on us.

There may be former rulers, presidents, or an emperor's image on coins, but we are made in God's image and we are to give Him our all. He has given us life, dominance over all creation, given us food, shelter, and the ability to love and be loved. This and more God gives us on a daily basis, yet we as Christians struggle with giving back to God. Why is that? Why do we have such an issue with control?

The second thing worth mentioning in regards to finances is also found in Mark 12:13-17, and we touched on it in the above paragraphs. Jesus says "Give to Caesar's what is Caesar's," but what is Caesar's? To get a better understanding, a little side note, and a short history lesson about Caesar and Rome around this time would be helpful.

Rome occupied most of the world, including Israel. Part of occupying a land was to instill Roman law and Roman taxes. So Rome had invaded and occupied the lands and commanded everyone to pay tax to Rome, but if not, there would be punishment.[62] Rome was also very protective of its empire, meaning that they would put down any and all who would try and conquer them.

So imagine what it would have been like for the Jews who were looking for a messiah and savior to come thinking that he would set up his earthly reign forever. This, of course, by logical deduction would mean that Rome would not be in charge anymore. Imagine their surprise when Jesus responded the way He did and told them to give to Caesar what was his.

---

[62] Rome was very well known for the sadistic and cruel punishment that they could inflict on a person. I could go into graphic detail about some of the ways that they would punish and torture people, but I do not think it necessary at this juncture.

Fast forward to today, what image is on our coins and bills? Whose authority are we under today in regards to an earthly rule? I know I hate taxes as much as the next guy, and I will be the first to say that they can be high or unfair at times, but we are commanded to pay them by Jesus. Even in Romans 13:7 it says how we are to pay taxes to whom taxes are owed, it cannot get much clearer than that.

It kills me every time I hear of Christians, pastors and religious figureheads not paying their taxes. Why are they trying to gyp the system? What can they accomplish by trying to get away with that kind of behavior? The only thing it does is drag the name of Jesus through the mud and dirty the Christian name and faith to the world around us.

The next part that I believe people struggle with in finances is that of being in debt. I know that there are times and seasons in our lives where debt can be inevitable, for example, during college or when buying a house. The problem comes when we start living outside our means and our reasonable debt starts becoming unreasonable.

Instead of a reliable car that gets you from point A to point B, you get a car that has the latest and greatest technology that gets you from point A to point B in 3.5 seconds and costs half a house to buy.

According to Sallie Mae in 2013, college students who are graduating are having an average of $3,156[63] in credit card charges.[64] Credit cards can be dangerous, they need to be used with care and caution. There are people that graduate with a college degree and struggle to make ends meet because of the burden of student loans and credit card debt.

I know and understand that this is a touchy subject, and I am in no way advocating that people stop attending college. However, what I am suggesting is that we focus on money management and to be smart with what God gives us. Let's look at what the Bible says about debt.

> Romans 13:8 says, "Owe no one anything, except to love each other, for the one who loves another has fulfilled the law."
>
> Romans 13:7 says, "Pay to all what is owed to them: taxes to whom taxes are owed, revenue to whom revenue is owed, respect to whom respect is owed, honor to whom honor is owed."
>
> Proverbs 22:7 says, "The rich rules over the poor, and the borrower is the slave of the lender."

---

[63] U.S Government Accountability Office, *CREDIT CARDS: Marketing to College Students Appears to Have Declined* (Washington, DC: GPO February 2014) http://www.gao.gov/assets/670/661121.pdf, 8.
[64] This number has been declining, but credit cards can be an easy temptation to fall into, yet not so easy to get out of.

These are just a few verses that touch on the subject of being in debt. I understand that debt happens in life, but we are to pay off our debt quickly so that we are not a slave to our lender. I know that actual slavery is not so much an issue in our society anymore. However, if left unchecked, debt can cause us to feel as if we were slaves.

As our checks and wages are garnished and debt collectors begin to bang down the door trying to regain what is owed to them, the pressure can build.

How is being in debt helpful? What does having these spending habits and situations of debt collectors look like to unsaved, unchurched, and lukewarm believers? Would this kind of situation be beneficial to your family or those close to you? If being financially burdened and being overwhelmed with debt is a reality for you right now, there is hope.

If you are in debt, do not get more credit cards, do not go shopping for extras, and do not take on more financial burden. Remember, give to God first, and then get out of debt. You cannot help others out if you are in trouble yourself.

Another part of being a responsible godly Christian is to have money in savings. There are some people that would argue that having a savings account is not relying on God, and they give verses such as:

Luke 12:24 says, "Consider the ravens: they neither sow nor reap, they have neither storehouse nor barn, and yet God feeds them. Of how much more value are you than the birds!"

Matthew 6:19-21 says, "'Do not lay up for yourselves treasures on earth, where moth and rust destroy and where thieves break in and steal, but lay up for yourselves treasures in heaven, where neither moth nor rust destroys and where thieves do not break in and steal. For where your treasure is, there your heart will be also.'"

These verses should not be taken as a "do not save your money," but rather, to have faith in God when hard times come. Rest and rely on God and his provisions, but use your head and the resources that he has given you. It is not to have our focus only on earthly items as stated in Matthew, but to remember that our treasure is in Heaven.

There are some verses in Proverbs that discuss how a wise man stores up and a good man leaves an inheritance.

Proverbs 21:20 says, "Precious treasure and oil are in a wise man's dwelling, but a foolish man devours it."

Proverbs 13:22 says, "A good man leaves an inheritance to his children's children, but the sinner's wealth is laid up for the righteous."

God gave us a brain for a reason. We are to be smart with our money and be able to give and save at the same time. This is not an excuse to hoard and be stingy. We should have a balance of having a savings and being able to give, both at the same time. It is easier said than done, trust me.

The extremes of either side of the financial coin, pardon the pun, are both unbiblical. To the one who squanders and spends money like their life depends on it is uncalled for and sinful. Yet the opposite is the one who saves everything and is never able to spend, give, or live generously.

Both are incorrect actions and both need to change. It is a hard balancing act and at times, we can be swayed to one side or the other, but we are to follow God, and no one said that would be easy.

Finally, when it comes to finances, Christians need to rely on God and be able to give all to Him, the good, the bad, and the confusing. God is not your personal accountant. He is not going to prepare your taxes or set up your 401K, but He will be there to help guide and strengthen you.

As a side note, please do not get yourself into situations where God is the only way out. What I mean is this, do not go buy a $200,000 car that you cannot afford and then say, "Well, God, I'm relying on you to make the payment." That is just dumb and irresponsible. It makes you look like a fool and will hurt you in the end. God is loving and God is giving, God will give you what you need.

We are to be responsible and smart on how we handle our finances and what we do with what God gives us. A Christian that is concerned with "keeping up with the Joneses" will eventually become ruined and will have missed some of the blessings of God. A politically correct Christian wanting to fit into this world will be stressed and worry their whole lives trying to figure out how to afford the latest and greatest and be just like everyone else.

Our treasure is not on this earth; it is in heaven. If you have a less than ideal car, but it gets you to where you are going, then rejoice because there are a lot of people that do not have that luxury. If you do not have the latest fashion line in your closet, just be thankful that you have clothes.

Always be thankful for what God has given even if it is not what you may want.[65] As the saying goes, there will always be someone with something better, so just be content.

If you are wanting to dive into this issue more, there are some authors that I recommend that include: Dave Ramsey, Larry Burkett, and Crown Financial Ministries. These guys specialize in financial matters and give biblical and practical support on how to manage your finances. I would encourage anyone to get their books if you struggle with money. Even if you do not, it can be beneficial to read up on how to handle what God has given to us.

A politically correct Christian gives change and leftovers to God; a Godly Christian will strive to honor what God has blessed them with and strive to give back to God faithfully. As I end this chapter, I am reminded of a saying that a friend of mine encourages people with. That saying is this, "You can never out-give God." Simple, yet profound. God has given and blessed us all so much already that anything we do in return is just a drop in the bucket by comparison.

---

[65] Sometimes I wonder if we even know what we want, or we are so inundated with commercials and salesmanship that we have lost our sense of what WE want and only know what THEY want us to want.

Discussion Questions

- What is your honest financial situation?
- What are some changes you could make?
- Where is your money going and towards what?
- Are you so consumed about keeping up with those around you that you forget about God?
- Do you struggle with keeping up appearances?
- What are some practical steps that you could take right now to better manage your budget?
- Are you willing to try and out-give God?

8

THE POLITICALLY CORRECT CHRISTIAN IN RELATIONSHIPS

The beauty of life is that it is full of relationships. The relationships between children and parents, between husband and wife, between employer and employee, friend and foe. Everywhere you look, there are relationships. So what are some of the differences between relationships and how is a Christian supposed to deal with them? How do we fall short and succumb to being politically correct with our relationships?

There is a verse that children learn very early on in Sunday school, VBS, or other children's church programs and it is found in Ephesians 6:1-3

> Children, obey your parents in the Lord, for this is right. Honor your father and mother that it may go well with you and that you may live long in the land.

One of the first relationships we have in our lives is the relationship we have with our parents. I like how this passage says parents and father and mother. What the passage does not say, is only your paternal parents, but it says whoever your parents are, children are to obey and honor.

This was a huge commandment for children, still is, but at the time this letter to the Ephesians was written, there was a lot of change happening to the world. Rome was starting its decent and slowly sliding backwards into history.

The book of Ephesians was written around 60 A.D. by Paul as he sat in a Roman prison. At the start of the Roman republic, before all the emperors, there was a term used in family life called Paterfamilias. This term literally meant father of the family, and the father wielded absolute power. The father of a family had final say, he could sell his family into slavery, kill his children, or even expel them from his family forever.

As the Roman Empire grew, the father lost a little of that power and laws were enacted to help protect the women and children, but the father still held the authority. This and other factors at this point had the Roman Empire beginning its decline and becoming morally bankrupt. It is at this point that Paul wrote the Ephesians telling children to obey and honor your parents.

I would like to take a second and point out how similar the social conditions we live in now are compared to the time of the Roman Empire. Even today, as children are being rebellious, having more control than they should, running around unsupervised and without consequence, the Bible hasn't changed. Children are to obey and honor their parents just as they should any person in authority.

While we are on this topic of parent/children relationships, I would like to talk to the parents about their relationships with their children. It is a two-way street, and there are some helpful guidelines and Biblical verses for parents as well.

Children are to obey and honor, but parents have a more difficult task. They are to teach and raise up children of God. What does that mean? What does that look like? Let's take some time and look at it. For those who do not have kids, rather they already have had them or are planning to have them, this part of the chapter will be beneficial and insightful to all of us.

In Proverbs 22:6 it says "Train up a child in the way he should go; even when he is old he will not depart from it."

This lays a heavy burden on parent's shoulders, the mom and dad are fully responsible for teaching their kids. This verse does not say, "Have children and the church and school system will teach your kids." I can hear the amen coming from all the pastors and youth workers now.

It *does* say, however, that God has commanded all parents to have the responsibility to train, instruct, and in general, be active in their children's lives. I have heard countless conversations and speeches about the issue with today's youth, and the one central issue that is often not brought up and the question that needs to be asked is this: Where are the parents? What are the parents doing?

The social norm in today's society is to have kids, give them to the school system, and you become a chaperone/photographer for their events. Half of the parents do not even know or care what their children are learning.

When a child commits suicide or threatens to blow up a school or shoots someone, the news interviews the parents, and a popular response is, "I never thought they could do that. I guess I never noticed." Sadly, I have heard interviews that sound like this all too often.

I want to make it clear at this point, and I say this with love and understanding to all parents: It is not someone else's job to raise your children, and it is not someone else's fault when your child goes on a rampage. The responsibility of your children falls squarely on your shoulders. God knows what you are going through, and He has given help through the Spirit on earth for you, but ultimately it is your responsibility as a parent to raise your children.

It should not be all doom and gloom for parents reading this. There are local churches with great youth programs that cannot wait to help you. This is what the local church is for, to come along side and help out on this journey through life.

There is another passage that I would like to address, and this deals more with the father, since we are taking time to discuss the parent relationship with children. It says back in Ephesians 6:4, "Fathers, do not provoke your children to anger, but bring them up in the discipline and instruction of the Lord."[66] I know how men are, we like to push the limit, we tease, and we torment and pick on each other, and sometimes this can go too far.

Fathers need to be like Christ; stern, but loving; kind, but not afraid to discipline; a leader, but willing to learn; humble, yet willing to stand for what is right. These are some of the qualities we as men, husbands, and fathers need to have. Unfortunately, this is not the reality.

---

[66] *The Holy Bible: New American Standard Bible.* Anaheim: Foundation Publications, 1995. Print.

The sad reality is that a majority of males in America are far from being men. What we are commanded to do and become as men and fathers is being swept away by golf, videogames, sports, friends, work, and a whole host of other endeavors that take us and our attention away from what we, as men, are called to do.[67] Sadly, this is how most men are behaving, nothing more than overgrown children, and so the responsibility of raising children falls on the wife, the mom.

Ephesians 6:4 clearly states that fathers are not supposed to provoke their kids to anger. What does that mean? It means that dads are not to give unreasonable commands or make a child do something that they cannot accomplish. It means holding your temper and not taking out frustration on your children. It means being aware of your child's limits and not always pushing their buttons.

The second half of the verse is where a lot of men fall short. Fathers are to bring them (children) up in discipline and instruction of the Lord. It is the father's job to discipline, and in my personal opinion, there is not enough appropriate discipline given anymore to our youth.

---

[67] These things and others are not bad in moderation, but when they creep in and steal or distort what we are called to do, it can then become a serious problem

When talking to my grandparents, or even my dad as I shared back in chapter one, I remember them telling me of how school teachers could spank unruly kids in the classroom. If a child acted up in school, they would get punished there at school, then the parent would discipline the child when they got home. My grandparents would finish by saying that they didn't have children shooting up schools back then because they knew what discipline was, and they had respect for the adults.

I remember as a child if I ever mouthed off or misbehaved, my mom would say, "Just wait until your dad gets home." I would always start to pray that they would forget or that the rapture would come before my dad got home. Sure enough, when dad got home, my mom would inform him of all my actions, and he would come to my room, and well, let's just say that I was a quick learner.

Where is the discipline? Where are the fathers? How has it come to this point where children are running the show, and the parents are just along for the ride? Fathers, give love and encouragement, but when the time comes that your child needs discipline, do it!

The last part of Ephesians 6:4 is about giving instruction of the Lord. Again it falls on you, dads, to be the leader and teacher of the house. It is not just the church's responsibility to teach the Bible to your children. The church is there to help and to offer assistance, but it is not only their job to train your child, it is *your* job.

Fathers have said before, "I just don't know much about the Bible." Well, pick it up and read it. If you do not know something, learn about it so that you can teach, or better yet, read the Bible with your children and your wife so that you all can learn together.

There are thousands of books out there that can help; ask your pastors to recommend some. If you don't have the money to buy them, then borrow them from your church library. They are there for exactly this reason. There is no excuse not to know or have the ability and resources to learn about God and His Word so that you can pass it on and teach your children.

I was fortunate growing up to have a father that was very knowledgeable not only in life, but in the Word of God. Even to this day, I will call him up and ask him about certain things that I might not understand or have a question about. I am not saying that my dad is perfect, but it is wonderful to know that if I ever have a question, I can ask my dad and either he will know the answer or help me find the answer.

Some are not that fortunate. The sad reality is that there are many children who do not have a father or mother. They grow up not knowing or having that love and support. The good news is that we have a Heavenly Father that will never leave us and will always be there to help, guide, protect, and love His little children.

A quick note to single mothers that may be reading this. Although I am not and could never fully understand what it would be like to be a single mother, please do not feel forgotten. Life can be hard and difficult, but that should never get in the way of being faithful to God and His Word. God is bigger than any problem that we may face. He is with you always, you are never alone, and you can do this!

Before I leave this particular aspect and we discuss other forms of relationships and what that looks like for a politically correct Christian and a true, authentic Christian, I want to mention one more thing regarding parents. Children are watching and paying attention to how the two of you interact with and react to each other. They base their perception of what a healthy relationship looks like from the two of you.

As a dramatic example and to get my point across, let's look at a politically correct Christian. Hypothetically, they could verbally abuse their spouse, yet in public be the most kind, courteous, and godly person around. Their children would pick up on this and then form their understanding that a good relationship can include abuse as long as it's in private.

To be in a good relationship they must be two-faced and fake in public and that verbal abuse is okay and acceptable, as long as it's in the home and not in public.

This is just an example, but you can easily see how the parents' actions and their relationship can impact their children's view and understanding of relationships with others for the rest of their lives.

It is so very important that we as parents and adults teach and train our children. Their whole life will depend on how they are trained. Raise them up in God's Word, teach them to find their identity in Jesus Christ, and to honor Him and obey His Word. Take a moment and ask yourself if you're doing everything you can to make sure that you are training and teaching our youth in God's Word.

Moving on through life, the next logical relationship that we come across is that of friendships and acquaintances. We as believers are all brothers and sisters in Christ. I want to take a moment and see what the Bible says about relationships with other Christians, our brothers and sisters.

> Hebrews 10:24-25 says, "And let us consider how to stir up one another to love and good works, not neglecting to meet together, as is the habit of some, but encouraging one another, and all the more as you see the day drawing near."

In this passage we see that we as believers are to stir up one another to love and do good works. I remember learning how to cook and bake from my mom and grandma. We would toss ingredients into a bowl and make sure we had the appropriate amounts of everything needed. Tossing ingredients into a bowl was only part of the cooking and baking process; however, it wasn't until we stirred everything together that we could move on to the baking and eventually the eating and enjoying of our treats.

Often in the Christian life we are quick to throw or toss some cheerful and encouraging words at someone as we pass by, but it is not until we take the time to stir them up that we can actually make a difference in their lives. It is not easy to make this kind of investment, and it is not the social norm.

In our society today, and our fast-paced environment, we want things instantly, even when it comes to spiritual matters, almost like a drive-thru. We pass by people in the halls or in an elevator, try to share something encouraging and stir them and encourage them to love, but it instead looks like this: "Hey, how ya doing? Good. You should love Jesus because I do. Okay! Have a great day, and I will pray for you."

A politically correct Christian will attend a church, but not really be a part of a church. What do I mean by that? As mentioned in Hebrews, it has become the habit of some to get into the habit of skipping church and neglecting the fellowship of believers. They are trading their God time and fellowship for TV time or sports time or fill-in-the-blank time.[68]

These types of Christians are the ones doing the drive-thru greetings and not really taking intentional time to grow, learn, follow, serve, or have a deep, godly relationship. We as believers are commanded to encourage each other in love.

I always get a kick out of the saying, "I don't have to go to church to love God." Really? Can you have a relationship with your spouse, significant other, best friend, or child without ever seeing them or talking to them. We need to be in regular meetings with God and other believers, make it a priority in your life.

God is always waiting to greet you and be with you. The question is: What is so important in your life that you would neglect the fellowship and relationship with the all-powerful, loving God? Why has it become so easy to put off attending church and gathering to fellowship with others, but not miss a Sunday morning or afternoon sporting event? It is a blessing not a burden to be part of the Christian faith.

---

[68] It is also important to note, that often a person can be at church physically but far from it mentally or spiritually. Don't assume that just because people are that that they are actually present.

For those who do attend and regularly meet, there are some verses that help us and give instruction on how to behave and how all Christians should live. These verses can help guide us in our everyday lives and also to help us identify when we, as Christians, have fallen into the temptation of being politically correct.

> Ephesians 4:29-32 says, "Let no corrupting talk come out of your mouths, but only such as is good for building up, as fits the occasion, that it may give grace to those who hear. And do not grieve the Holy Spirit of God, by whom you were sealed for the day of redemption. Let all bitterness and wrath and anger and clamor and slander be put away from you, along with all malice. Be kind to one another, tenderhearted, forgiving one another, as God in Christ forgave you."

Many of us are familiar with this passage of scripture. It has been in numerous sermons and been the topic of many youth pastors' messages. This passage is so well known, yet it is one that we seem to forget about all the time, even in its simplest form. I would like to briefly dissect this passage and break it down for application in our lives.

Unwholesome talk (some translations render it as corrupt talk) should not come out of our mouths. I like the word unwholesome because I believe that it is more encompassing and includes a host of unbeneficial chatter.

We should only open our mouths and speak if it will help others and benefit those who are listening. It does not mean benefit them by sharing the latest gossip or spreading the juiciest rumors.

In every church and at many prayer meetings, if you listen long enough, you will hear something to this effect, "I want to pray for so and so because they did this and that and they are struggling with this list of items that I have brought to the church today on their behalf…" You know what I'm talking about, the latest and greatest gossip in the form of a prayer. As I was told repeatedly as a child, "If you do not have anything nice to say, then do not say anything at all."

Society thrives on gossip. Look at any tabloid at your grocery store, often times they are full of the latest celebrity gossip. There are entire television shows dedicated to this sort of endeavor. There is nothing wrong with discussing or learning about a person, but there is a fine line between that and gossiping. As Christians we must not gossip. It is difficult and challenging because of how we are wired, and it can be masked as being many different things, such as a prayer request.

Again, we are to build up our fellow believers with our conversation and not bring them down. I want to quickly mention that we are to build up, but that does not mean that we color everything rosy with our speech, be truthful and honest. If a believer is in the wrong, then let them know, but with love and a tender heart. If someone messes up, we should not rub it in their face and broadcast it around the entire planet.[69] Rather, we should go to them and help them up and keep going on our journey through life, together as brothers and sisters in Christ.

Verse 31 of Ephesians chapter 4 seems a little out of place, right? I mean, Christians do not get angry. We are supposed to be happy, care-free and never have problems, right? Wrong! We all are human, and as such, we have our own issues and problems to deal with. There will be struggle, pain, anger, and confrontation because we are all imperfect humans trying to get along with each other.

Paul was very exact in writing this passage. He knew what was happening in the church then and what would, could, and has happened in the church today. Some of the fiercest battles I have witnessed have been within the walls of a church. They were almost willing to shed blood and die because one group liked the carpet blue and the other group liked the carpet brown.

---

[69] You social media junkies know what I am talking about. There could be a massive amount of books written about how social media spreads gossip, false information, and negativity has ruined people's lives. Christians should never be a part of that kind of thing.

This type of behavior happens in almost every church at one time or another. Rest assured, even if you do not see it, it happens. It might be over what flowers to plant out front, what music to play, not play on Sunday, or how the youth group needs more or less funding. These are issues that will draw out the warriors, gossipers, and drama makers, resulting in sides being taken and the church being negatively affected.

Take a step back and look at this scene, it is no wonder the world looks at the church and laughs. Why would anyone want to join a group of people that claim the love of Jesus, but will fight to the death over how the worship leader played Amazing Grace or how the nursery was painted?

I understand many of you like the color blue, many like the music loud, others love tulips out front instead of roses. Is it really that important that you would ruin relationships, that you would make yourself look like a fool and a hot head? Re-read verse 31, please.

If we are truly followers of Christ, then we need to get over ourselves and get on board with the love of God. If we call ourselves the family of God, then act like it! Stop holding that grudge, stop whispering behind that person's back trying to stir up trouble, stop trying to recruit people to your side of the argument, and stop being angry and hateful towards everyone who is not just like you.

A true Christian would put a stop to this kind of behavior and try to resolve and overcome that kind of thinking, for the good of the body of Christ. A politically correct Christian would try and take sides and perpetuate this attitude, which needs to be dealt with immediately.

Verse 32 sums it up with how we should be. We are to be kind to everyone, tender hearted, believing the best and having an open heart to others. The kicker is this: Forgive one another. Why? Because God, who is holy and perfect, came to die on the cross for you, for me, and for the people who painted the nursery pink instead of salmon.

Christ died for everyone! We tend to forget what God has done for us in our little, petty arguments and disagreements. It's as if God was on our side only. We tend to forget that in God's eyes we are all sinners and worthy of hell, regardless of how good we are or how well we fought and got our way. We are all on the same side, and we all need to get along. It will be hard, long and tedious, but it will be so worth it in the end.

Sometimes it seems as if the church is full of little groups or friends, little clichés that only get along with each other. We are not called to live in our little bubble surrounded by people that only agree with us. We need to spend time with the family of God. Yes, even the ones that have caused arguments and disagreements.

As a side note, the Bible does talk about having good friends to hang out with in Proverbs 13:20. Choose your friends wisely. Your friends will shape you and change you, maybe not completely, but they will have an impact on you. How often do we do things we might not do by ourselves but will do them with friends?

Part of being a friend is being accountable. What I mean is a good friend will also be your accountability partner. If you do not have a person that you could call at any time with a need, then you do not have a friend.

We tend to downplay the need for an accountability partner, and I know why. It is uncomfortable to have them call us out, or it can be painful and humiliating to confide certain things to them. But how great is it when the relationship is there and they come alongside to help out when we are in our weakest state and in most need of help.

A good friend will be there for you, a good friend will call you out when you are straying from the faith, and a good friend will have your back in love and encourage you in your journey. Are you a good friend? Do you have a good friend?

The next logical step as we move through the relationships from friendship is making the choice of moving from friend to companion and then to dating and marriage.

One of the hardest things about dating is figuring out if the two of you are a fit or not and if you can spend the rest of your life with each other.

2 Corinthians 6:14 says, "Do not be unequally yoked with unbelievers. For what partnership has righteousness with lawlessness? Or what fellowship has light with darkness?"

Generally, when we think about this verse, we apply it to whether or not a person is Christian. I want to go a step further and apply it this way: Just because two people are Christian does not mean that they are equally yoked.

What do I mean by that? Well, a yoke is a wooden harness that fit two oxen or donkeys to pull a cart. These animals had to be of equal size and strength in order for them to work together and pull the cart. Spiritually speaking, when you find that special someone to date and potentially marry, make sure you are both of the same mind and have the same resolve in the faith.

A relationship will not work if you two are on separate pages as far as faith, beliefs and life goals. Now don't misunderstand, I am not saying find a mirror image of yourself and date them. I am not saying that differences cannot be worked out or overcome. I am simply saying that if there is a strong Christian and a weak Christian in the relationship, it is easier to pull someone down than to lift them up, so be careful. Just like iron sharpens iron, so one spouse, or potential spouse, must be able to sharpen the other in marriage and in the Christian faith.

This leads me to a side note for the ladies. The "bad boy" image can be very appealing and fun, but it is not always beneficial. I understand that you believe the best in them and that you can "change them" and everything will work out. Sadly, this is not a romance comedy and the chances of that happening are slim.

I do have some friends that have had luck with the bad boy thing and it worked out and the guys have changed their ways and are very influential in the ministry, but it was God working on them and in them that caused the change, not their girlfriends. It is only through the transforming power of God and His Holy Spirit that one can truly change.

For sake of conversation, I also want to point out that this is the exception, not the standard. I know this because of what it says in 1 Corinthians 15:33 "Do not be misled: Bad company corrupts good character."[70]

For other scriptures on how company or friends can ruin your character, morals, and life. Just read through Proverbs, it is full of verses dealing with relationships.

---

[70] *The New International Version*. Grand Rapids, MI: Zondervan, 2011. Print.

The next thing to talk about that always gets brought up when dealing with dating is having the sex talk. The sex talk, how uncomfortable, how awkward, how embarrassing, yet how necessary it is to remind ourselves and those who are with us of the dangers of "fooling around" outside of marriage.

When did it become taboo to talk about sex? I am not arguing for the crude jokes and explicit detail, but whatever happened to open, honest discussion about something that consumes the average person's mind more often than almost anything else?

Parents, please do not be naïve. We have all been there and dealt with the temptation. Take time and lay down some ground rules to help steer and guide your children through such dangerous territory. This is all part of guiding and training children. Remember, a politically-correct-Christian parent will try and conform and be their friend. You must not be their friend, you must be their parent.

It is also extremely important that parents try and keep open lines of communication with their children and teens, having open and honest discussions with them. A parent that is unaware and doesn't care about their children's actions will soon be a grandparent taking care of their children's children.

For those of you dating and outside your parent's homes, I will assume that you are old enough to make your own decisions. However, when the urge strikes, it is hard to make good decisions. There has been research conducted that shows, scientifically, that there are certain chemicals, vasopressin for men and oxytocin for women, that are released during, and even before the act of having sex. These chemicals aid the bonding process between two people.

This chemical conveys the idea of trust and establishes a permanent bond with the other person, hence why it can be so painful when people have sex before marriage and then end their relationship. These chemicals can be caused by other physical forms of expression as well.[71] That is why it is good to take a second and be proactive (this is for both guys and girls).

Please take a second and read these passages.

> 1 Thessalonians 4:3-5 says, "For this is the will of God, your sanctification: that you abstain from sexual immorality; that each one of you know how to control his own body in holiness and honor, not in the passion of lust like the Gentiles who do not know God."

---

[71] McIlhaney, Joe S., and Freda McKissic Bush. *Hooked: New Science on How Casual Sex Is Affecting Our Children*. Chicago: Northfield Pub., 2008. Print.

1 Corinthians 6:18 says, "Flee from sexual immorality. Every other sin a person commits is outside the body, but the sexually immoral person sins against his own body."

The Bible talks a lot about sexual immorality. Do a study on it, and you will find numerous verses dealing with this subject. What the Bible doesn't give is a lot of practical advice to help stop things from happening before they get too far.

Here are a few helpful tips:

- Don't be alone in a dark room
- Go on group dates
- Do not just sit around on a couch alone
- Do not hang out in the bedroom
- If you are tired, do not hang out with the other person
- Do not lay down together (duh!)
- Don't place yourself in a compromising situation
- No closed doors
- Do not play games that elicit touching

The list could go on and on, so maybe take a moment to write some of your own down on a sheet of paper, and establish some ground rules that both parties can agree on. Parents, do not hesitate to chat with your children and help them to understand your rules; it is for their own good and they will thank you later in life.

Stick to these guidelines no matter what. It will be difficult and it can be easy to just push them to the side, but it is not worth it.

After the dating relationship comes the marriage relationship. There are many good books available for a person to read, and I would encourage people thinking about marriage or who are already married to read them. Some that my wife and I have enjoyed reading are:

- *Preparing for Marriage: Discover God's Plan for a Lifetime of Love.*[72]
- *The 5 Love Languages: the Secret to Love that Lasts*[73]
- *Real Marriage: the Truth about Sex, Friendship and Life Together.*[74]

---

[72] Boehi, David, and Dennis Rainey. *Preparing for Marriage*. Ventura, CA: Gospel Light, 2010. Print.
[73] Chapman, Gary. *The 5 Love Languages: The Secret to Love that Lasts*. Chicago, Il: Northfield Publishing, 1992. Print.
[74] Driscoll, Mark, and Grace Driscoll. *Real Marriage: The Truth about Sex, Friendship & Life Together*. Nashville, TN Thomas Nelson, 2012. Print.

- *Love and Respect: the Love She Most Desires, the Respect He Desperately Needs.*[75]

There are many other good books out there that can help with whatever situation you are in with regards to marriage. Ask your local pastor for recommendations on what to read or how he can help you in your stage of life. Many churches offer classes for seriously dating and engaged couples, and you can talk to your pastor about some of these options as well.

One thing I know for sure is this, if a couple doesn't place God at the center of their relationship, then they will not have a fulfilling relationship. A couple that prays together stays together. It is not just a cliché but actual truth. There have been many times in my marriage where there was nothing we could do but pray. However, as a word of encouragement and personal testimony, God is always faithful, and He will never leave or forget his children.

There is a lot of garbage flying around America in regards to marriage. It has become acceptable and even the norm for a person to get divorced. Even in the church and in Christian circles today, we have bought into the idea that divorce is okay. This is just not acceptable.

---

[75] Eggerichs, Emerson. *Love & Respect: The Love She Most Desires, the Respect He Desperately Needs.* Nashville, TN: Integrity, 2004. Print.

In America today 50% percent of first marriages end in divorce, 67% of second marriages and 73% of third marriages end in divorce.[76] This number increases even more for couples that cohabitate before marriage. Different polls and different surveys might vary from a percent to another, but the point remains: Marriage is not sacred anymore. No one is in it for the long haul, and popular thought is that if you are not happy, then just get out.

I know what you are thinking, that these statistics cover all of America and not just Christians. Well, according to a recent Barna Survey, almost a third of Christians who attend church at least once a week will end their marriage in divorce.[77] George Barna also noted that we as Americans have grown comfortable with the notion of divorce, as if it were a natural part of life. Christians are no exception.

It has become politically correct and acceptable to get divorced. Sadly, we as Christians have allowed this to happen, and worse, allowed this to enter our beliefs. We have become so worried about being politically correct that we do not take a stand against divorce.

Matthew 19:9 says, "And I say to you: 'whoever divorces his wife, except for sexual immorality, and marries another, commits adultery.'" It grieves God when a couple goes

---

[76] Divorce Statistics, www.divorcestatistics.org accessed 2016
[77] Barna Research Group LTD, 2016

through a divorce. He did not intend for marriage to end like that. Until death do us part has been taken out of many marriage vows today. It is extremely sad and painful when a person goes through a divorce, more so as a Christian.

If you have gone through a divorce before or are going through one now, my heart goes out to you. I have never been through one, but I have seen the effects it has on the family and all who are involved.

I agree that there are some circumstances where divorce can be justified, such as sexual immorality or abuse. However, we must strive to follow God's Word and apply it to our lives. Remember, God is able to help us and empower us to overcome all the circumstances that we might face.

If you are struggling in your marriage, please seek help and counseling. Take the time and effort to work through whatever problems the both of you are facing. It will be hard and it will hurt, it will take time to recover, and it will take a lot of forgiveness, but it will be incredibly worth it in the end.

A marriage is never easy, it requires work, lots of work from *both* sides. Just do not give up. God is here to help, and your fellow brothers and sisters in Christ are here to help.

We as Christians should not buy into the social norm; a politically correct Christian will follow society's trends and not go against the grain. We are commanded to follow God and His Word, which includes marriage.

We are to help and love those who are struggling and show them God's love and help them to correct their mistakes and persevere through life. We are all in this together.

Christianity is not a religion, it is a relationship with Jesus Christ who died on the cross and paid the ultimate price. While Jesus was here on the earth, He spent so much time developing relationships because it was (still is) one of the most important aspects of Christianity and of following God.

God has a perfect relationship in heaven called the Trinity. He wants a relationship with us and wants us to have relationships with our fellow man.

> 1 John 4:20 says, "If anyone says, 'I love God,' and hates his brother, he is a liar; for he who does not love his brother whom he has seen cannot love God whom he has not seen."

Relationships take work and prayer. It is not easy, but no matter what relationships we have or find ourselves in, we are to be more and more like Jesus and show His love though these relationships. What kind of struggles are you having in relationships? How can you pray for the relationship? What steps can be taken to mend any broken or damaged relationships?

One of the hardest aspects of any relationship is the act of forgiveness. It can be easy to talk about and it can be easy to apply, in theory, yet to live it out and put into the practical outworking of our lives is another thing entirely.

I have met with people and couples before that have had some issues arise, and one of the first responses that I hear is something like this, "Well, I am just not sure if I can forgive, you just wouldn't understand." Sometimes they are right, I would not understand, yet I know one who does.

I know God understands sin more fully than you or I ever will, and it is normally at this juncture that I kindly remind them about God.

God being God knows everything, past, present, and future. Knowing every single one of our lives fully with all our "dirty little secrets" still sent His own son to die on the cross and offer us the forgiveness and hope of salvation. So yes, I think that He would understand about all that has been done and could ever be done by a human, because when we sin, we sin against God, and yet, He still forgives.

If you are a Christian, we are to be like Christ. Because Christ forgives and offers forgiveness, how much more should we strive to offer forgiveness to those who have done us wrong? The Bible is full of scripture commanding us to do so. I am not saying that forgiveness is easy, but it is necessary.

A politically correct Christian harbors ill feelings because it is socially acceptable. A true Christian forgives.

Discussion Questions

- What is one relationship or aspect of your relationship you can work on?
- What are some practical steps to have a healthy relationship with your spouse, child, parent, friend, co-worker, or boss?
- Are you struggling with forgiveness?
- What would it look like to truly forgive someone who has wronged you?

Mark Taylor

CONCLUSION

Hopefully, as you have read through this book you have been encouraged, challenged, and aware of what it looks like to be a politically correct Christian and what it looks like to be a committed follower of Jesus Christ. My prayer is that you not just forget about this book as you leave it on your shelf, but that you strive to live out a God-filled, God-centered life.

We all can become trapped and allured into being a politically correct Christian, forgetting what we know we should do, and trading it all in for what people are telling us to do. We have all fallen victim to this; however, now is the time to make the commitment to live an intentional Christ-focused life.

I intentionally wrote this book in a way that will be helpful, as it is easy to read, understand, and apply to our everyday lives. My prayer is that you will read this book and dive deeper into what it looks like to live an authentic Christian life.

There are a few items that I would like to address before leaving you and that is the matter of judgment, forgiveness, and encouragement.

The temptation of judgment comes after we have learned something and began applying it to our lives. We tend to look down or think condemning thoughts towards others who are not doing as we do. We fall victim to temptation by passing judgment on those who are not like us.

Consequently, when we are passing judgment in an unbiblical manner, we are causing ourselves to be prideful and puffed up. Do not misunderstand me, there can be cause to judge a person's actions, but it is to be done in a loving way and handled in a biblical manner.

The judging that I am talking about is the kind of judgment that we are most familiar with. Sometimes it can sound something like this: "Well I am just glad that I do not drink like *they* do, that is simply just awful, I will be praying for them." Now, praying for them is not a bad thing, we are supposed to do it, but not from the standpoint of being glad you are not like them.

During the time of Jesus in Jewish culture, it was noted that often times the more "religious" people would pray and thank God that they were not like others who struggled with (fill in the blank) sin.

The ironic thing was that they were then being filled up with pride because they saw themselves as being less of a sinner.

As a Christian and follower of Christ, we are to offer forgiveness. We cannot hold such attitudes of anger, bitterness, resentment or any such emotional baggage towards another fellow believer; we must forgive.

Ephesians 4:31-32 states, "Let all bitterness and wrath and anger and clamor and slander be put away from you, along with all malice. Be kind to one another, tenderhearted, forgiving one another, as God in Christ forgave you."

There are numerous verses dealing with the topic of forgiveness and how we, as Christians, are to follow the example of Christ and offer forgiveness. It is refreshing to know that God will be the ultimate judge and we will not have to worry about it.

To forgive someone can be difficult, but so worth it in the end. By forgiving a person of their actions and what they have done, it allows you as the forgiver to be free from their hold over you.

Let me explain. Say for a moment that a person in your church seems to always be in the way and gets under your skin. As you live your life and try to faithfully serve the Lord, they just seem to do everything against you.

You have several options that present themselves towards resolving this situation.

- Fight fire with fire, meaning that if they are saying false things against you, your family, or your ministry, you make certain that you tell more people the dirt about them.

- Harbor your pent-up feelings and frustrations, keeping it inside and pretending that it doesn't bother you until you have a nervous breakdown or burnout. The other causality in the aftermath of harboring feelings and emotions can be your family. You can very quickly get on a nasty cycle of events that can be very difficult to get off of.

- Go to them and politely discuss your concerns, perceptions and feelings about them. They may have some legitimate issues that you are unaware of. At any rate, no matter the outcome, offer forgiveness. Even if they refuse and do not want your forgiveness, give it to them and move on in your life.

When we as believers offer forgiveness, we are doing what is biblical and what is healthy for us in our walk with Christ. It also removes the power from the other person. Power, you ask? Yes, power. See, the first two options do great harm to you and your spirit by giving them the power to inflict harm to you. If you forgive them, then there can be no harmful thought or actions because you are willing to say, "I love you and I forgive you." The rest is then left up to God.

Forgiveness is difficult and hard to accomplish. It is much easier to talk about and discuss in theory than it is to put into practice. However, the rewards of offering true forgiveness are incredible.

A politically correct Christian fights fire with fire, and they sink down to the level of their antagonist. They also are some of the first people to point out and exploit others' faults and failures. This is not biblical and should not be done. My prayer for you is that after reading this book you will be able to identify this kind of behavior and overcome it.

We cannot be perfect, we all sin, no one is above temptation and failure and that is why we must forgive and allow God and the Holy Spirit to work in people's lives. We are not the religious police, it is not our job to walk around highlighting and building a case against people and of their faults. Encouragement, love, and forgiveness is the name of this game.

Encouragement is something seriously lacking in some Christian circles. I have been in some churches that have a death-camp feel more than an eternal life feeling. You know what I am talking about? No one smiles, the pastor is all doom and gloom, and the people in the church act like they are in prison instead of acting like they have been set free.

Encouragement, realistic encouragement, is an important aspect of the Christian life. Looking at 1 Thessalonians 5:9-11 which says, "For God has not destined us for wrath, but to obtain salvation through our Lord Jesus Christ, who died for us so that whether we are awake or asleep, we might live with him. Therefore, encourage one another and build one another up, just as you are doing." You can see how we must encourage and build each other up.

What does encouragement and building others up look like? It can be as simple as inviting them out to coffee or writing them a short note of encouragement. If you are really wanting to encourage them, maybe take them out to eat or give a gift card to their family. Encouragement doesn't have to be expensive, it is just simply something that will spur on the person to becoming more like Christ, with a highlight of what positive things they have been doing.

There can be some encouragement that allows for areas of improvement in their Christian life. However, in my opinion, if you are willing to take the time to point out areas in a person's life that need improvement, I think that you should also be willing to help them understand what the Bible says and assist/guide them through their improvement process. Taking time to see what they are doing and *how* they are doing will of course lead to more encouragement and a deeper relationship with that person.

Encouragement is such a blessing. I mean let's face it, who doesn't like to receive some words of affirmation and hear great job. As you are reading this, take some time and focus on a person that you know that could use some encouragement.

The thing about encouragement is that it is not something that can be done when we are self-centered. We have to be looking at others and noticing them and what they are doing. We have to be selfless and be focused on others, not in a critical way, but in ways that allow us opportunities to comfort, build up and encourage other believers.

A politically correct Christian buys into the idea of "It's all about me!" They think that it is all about what the church and Christianity can do for them. This is not a correct way of thinking at all. We should be so focused on others that we often forget ourselves. I am reminded of a passage of scripture found in Acts.

> Acts 2:42-47 says, "And they devoted themselves to the apostles' teaching and the fellowship, to the breaking of bread and the prayers. And awe came upon every soul, and many wonders and signs were being done through the apostles. And all who believed were together and had all things in common. And they were selling their possessions and belongings and distributing the proceeds to all, as any had need. And day by day, attending the temple together and breaking bread in their homes, they received their

food with glad and generous hearts, praising God and having favor with all the people. And the Lord added to their number day by day those who were being saved."

Notice how the church was so devoted to the teaching and fellowship that they could not help but notice the needs of others? Sounds weird, right? They were so focused on God that they started noticing the needs of those around them. When we as believers devote ourselves to the teaching of God and allow it to work in us, we become more aware of our need to do what God has commanded and taught us.

Notice what their response was in verse 45 of Acts chapter 2. They were selling what they had and giving it to those in need. Now, if I were in need, nothing would be more encouraging and demonstrative of God's love than to have someone sell what they had in order to give to me. Talk about encouragement and selflessness.

Imagine what this world would look like if we, as Christians, practiced what the Bible says. What would people think if we gave until it hurt? Imagine if we forgave others instead of getting even. What would happen if we all sought for unity instead of fighting and bickering over the littlest, insignificant things?

What would the world think? What would those who have bought into the lie that Christians have to be politically correct think? What would happen if we as believers took a stand for Christ in our daily lives?

My hope is that you use this book to make notes, highlight sections, and have conversations so that you can take some of these practices and live it out.

There is a quote that I heard from a pastor of mine when I was younger that has stuck with me through the years, and it is this: "Knowledge can change your mind, but application can change your life." It is not about how much you can learn in a book, but rather how much of the book you can use in your life.

This entire book cannot be lived out at once, but spend some time focusing on select chapters and applying them to your life. Get your group of friends together and consciously work on these areas so that we all can become better, more obedient children of God and not fall victim to the lie that we must fit into the world and become politically correct by forgetting the message of God's Word.

I will leave you with this verse from Romans 12:1-2

> I appeal to you therefore, brothers, by the mercies of God, to present your bodies as a living sacrifice, holy and acceptable to God, which is your spiritual worship. Do not be conformed to this world, but be transformed by the renewal of your mind, that by testing you may discern what is the will of God, what is good and acceptable and perfect.

God Bless

Mark Taylor

NOTES

Boehi, David, and Dennis Rainey. *Preparing for Marriage.* Ventura, CA: Gospel Light, 2010. Print.

Barna Research Group LTD. Barna.org. Retrieved March 22, 2016 from barna.org website: https://www.barna.org/

Chapman, Gary. The 5 Love Languages: The Secret to Love that Lasts. Chicago, Il: Northfield Publishing, 1992. Print.

Driscoll, Mark, and Grace Driscoll. *Real Marriage: The Truth about Sex, Friendship & Life Together.* Nashville, TN: Thomas Nelson, 2012. Print.

Divorce Statistics. divorcestatistics.org. Retrieved March 22, 2016 from divorcestatistics.org website: Http://www.divorcestatistics.org

Eggerichs, Emerson. *Love & Respect: The Love She Most Desires, the Respect He Desperately Needs.* Nashville, TN: Integrity, 2004. Print.

Farris, Michael. *What a Daughter Needs From Her Dad.* 2004 Bethany House Publishers, Bloomington, MN. Print.

Idleman, Kyle. *God's at War: Defeating the Idols That Battle for Your Heart.* Grand Rapids, MI: Zondervan, 2013.

James Dobson. (n.d.). AZQuotes.com. Retrieved February 29, 2016, from AZQuotes.com Web site: http://www.azquotes.com/quote/952000

Lind, Bill. "The Origins of Political Correctness," *Accuracy in Academia* (2000), http://www.academia.org/the-origins-of-political-correctness/

Liptak, Adam. "Supreme Court Ruling Makes Same-Sex Marriage a Right Nationwide." *The New York Times*, June 26, 2015. http://www.nytimes.com/2015/06/27/us/supreme-court-same-sex-marriage.html?_r=0.

McIlhaney, Joe S., and Freda McKissic Bush. *Hooked: New Science on How Casual Sex Is Affecting Our Children.* Chicago: Northfield Pub., 2008. Print.

Merriam-Webster's Collegiate Dictionary. Springfield, MA: Merriam-Webster, 2009. Print.

Miller, Rhea, George Shea, "I'd Rather Have Jesus" in *The Celebration Hymnal, Songs and Hymns for Worship*, Edited by Tom Fettke, Ken Barker, Camp Kirkland, 506. USA: Word/Integrity, 1997. Print.

New International Version. Colorado Springs, CO: International Bible Society, 1984. Print.

Planned Parenthood Annual Report 2012-2013. Report. New York: Planned Parenthood, 2013. http://www.plannedparenthood.org

Starnes, Todd. "NBC Omits "God" From Pledge of Allegiance...Again." *Fox News*, January 8, 2015.

http://www.foxnews.com/opinion/2015/01/08/nbc-omits-god-from-pledge-allegiance-again.html.

The Holy Bible: New American Standard Bible. Anaheim: Foundation Publications, 1995. Print.

U.S. Census Bureau (2010) Retrieved from http://www.census.gov/2010census/.

U.S. Department of Education, National Center for Education Statistics, *The Condition of Education 2009* (Washington, DC: GPO, 2009) http://nces.ed.gov/pubs2009/2009081.pdf.

U.S. Department of Labor, Bureau of Labor Statistics, *American Time Use Survey, 2014 Results* (Washington, DC: June 24, 2015) http://www.bls.gov/news.release/pdf/atus.pdf.

U.S Government Accountability Office, *CREDIT CARDS: Marketing to College Students Appears to Have Declined* (Washington, DC: GPO February 2014): 8. http://www.gao.gov/assets/670/661121.pdf

Varnum v. Brien. 2009, 07-1499. Iowa District Court. http://www.iowacourts.gov/wfData/files/Varnum/07-1499(1).pdf

ABOUT THE AUTHOR

Mark Taylor has been in various ministry positions for over a decade serving in both small and large churches. He has earned multiple degrees with the most recent being his Master of Divinity from Midwestern Baptist Theological Seminary. He currently is the Church Consultant for Text In Church and is a minister for the Fort Leavenworth Army Base. He enjoys spending time with his wife and family.